Masud and Humanity

Faqadt Wawujadat

Julian Ashbourn

This book is dedicated to the many thousands of orphans who are being generated by a world which calls itself 'civilised' and to all those who do their best to care for and accommodate them, both in orphanages and as foster parents. These poor children are, through no fault of their own, are often destined to start along their own journey of life without the love and support of their own family.

Contents

Origins

The clouds were slowly rolling over the tops of the Asir mountains where Masud was walking, close to his home town of Abha. It was a magical moment when Masud found himself totally engulfed by the clouds, which seemed to draw him into their midst as if wishing to communicate with him. He sat down and watched in wonder as the mist swirled around him before slowly moving on. At that moment, the sun suddenly broke through the higher clouds and shone its rays down directly on to the mountain tops, creating areas of brightness and shadows as one or two lower clouds lingered on.

Masud wished that his family could be there with him at that moment, especially his bride to be Aaliyah and his young sister Nora whom he knew would be enchanted by this experience. His Father, Abdul Rahman would no doubt just nod quietly, while his lovely Mother Nadia would have smiled benevolently at them as she always did when her family were around her and happy. It was indeed a special moment which filled Masud's heart with happy thoughts of the natural world around him. A world which he knew intimately and loved intensely. He was never happier than when roaming across the hills, climbing the mountains and dropping down into the wadis in order to appreciate the many contrasts of nature's wonderful creations with which he was so liberally surrounded, kama 'arad Allah.

Having found a convenient rock upon which to sit and gaze at the beauty surrounding him, Masud rested for a while and started to wonder about how many other men had climbed this same mountain and had a similar experience, perhaps thousands of years ago. No doubt they had also been in awe of Allah's beautiful designs and the beautiful sights which he gave to those who understood. But who would these men have been? And how many may have passed upon this very mountain trail before him? Where would they have been going and for what purpose? Such thoughts flooded into Masud's consciousness and filled him with a desire to understand more about the human species, of which he was of course a member.

Masud was already aware that, in Neolithic times, just following the last glaciation, there were people scattered all over the world, in Europe, the British Isles, the Nordic countries and Russia, the Middle East, Asia and South East Asia, Australasia, Africa, India and beyond. However, these peoples, united in time, were somewhat disunited with regard to their level of capabilities. At least, it seemed on the surface to be this way and yet, even in the least expected areas, great feats of engineering or personal endurance have become evident. It is also clear that, in Neolithic times, there was a complex web of trade routes which existed and which seemed to cover almost all of the known world. The same people who stood where Masud was now standing, themselves, would have probably travelled across North Africa, back across Sinai and into the Arabian Peninsula from where they would follow their stars in either an easterly, southerly or northerly direction, maybe taking years to complete their journey before, once more, embarking on this great adventure. Masud considered the nomadic life style and envied them their freedom for, although their life was sometimes hard, they were truly free and travelled wherever they wished in pursuit of trade and adventure.

But then, thought Masud, from where did these nomadic tribes come from and how was it that the ancient world was so relatively connected? It was indeed a subject most intriguing and one which sat quietly upon Masud's mind and would not go. He rose from his rocky perch and continued to walk in the mountains, appreciating the beauty of the natural world surrounding him, while simultaneously wondering how the human species came to spread so effectively and so quickly during Neolithic times and, even before in Mesolithic times for which archaeologists are continuing to find much evidence of human activity. This confirms the presence of humans from 10,000 years BC and, in fact, from well before that time as, by the Mesolithic period, humans were already quite advanced, with intelligently conceived and built homes, refined spears and other weapons with which to hunt and also an aesthetic which often shows itself among the various trinkets and ornaments found at burial sites. This suggested to Masud that our knowledge of human evolution was only limited by our ability to look back far enough. He was aware of the claim of finding human remains in Canada which were dated to around 20,000 years ago. This sits comfortably with the legends handed down among the First Nations people of their own history in the area.

Masud reluctantly returned home and discussed his musing with Aaliyah who similarly became very interested in the origins of the human species. It was a challenging idea, for there existed many claims and counter claims and yet, we are still missing the 'missing link' as it had been claimed since Victorian times. Many remains found within the fossil record and claimed to have been of hominids, were later confirmed to be those simply of apes.

The term 'hominid' refers to the zoological group known as Hominidae which, in turn leads on to the various Australopithecus and Homo strands which would seem to lead to our current Homo sapiens species. Although, even this lineage has some areas of doubt associated with it. However, Masud was satisfied that the Hominidae group were most probably our ancestors. Perhaps the most famous remains from the period is the skeleton of 'Lucy' the hominid found by Donald Johanson and Tom Gray in 1974 at the site of Hadar in Ethiopia. These remains have been dated to over three million years of age. Examples of Australopithecus have been found in the East African area and have been dated back to a similar period of around three million years ago. However, as Masud observed, these were clearly not of the human species but more closely related to Chimpanzees. It seems that they could walk upright, should they so wish, just as most modern apes can.

The various archaeological finds from this period, while being fascinating enough, were not comparable with Homo sapiens. They were far more primitive. That many have been found in East Africa, simply reflects that this is the area of most interests to archaeologists and is an area which is easily excavated. This is what had led to the 'out of Africa' theory which is significantly flawed in light of other discoveries and which, in any event, is unlikely given the genetic variety of early humans and their diverse geographic dispersion. Indeed, it is unlikely that we evolved genetically from a common ancestor as this often does not occur in natural evolution. Instead, nature often produces a group of similar organisms, from which a smaller group will eventually succeed. Furthermore it often does this in a geographically dispersed pattern. This explains why there are genetically distinct variations of many species, including humans, distributed geographically. When this occurs, the various groups tend to evolve according to their own local conditions. In the modern world, the human species are becoming less geographically separated and far more mixed. Mixed breeding creates hybrids which inherit the characteristics of both parent species and will then continue to evolve according to the conditions that they find themselves living in.

Darwin's Finches

The second voyage of HMS Beagle set off in December 1831 with the young Naturalist Charles Darwin on board, something which appealed to Commander Robert FitzRoy as he wanted someone on the voyage who had a knowledge of Geology and the Natural Sciences. When the ship visited the Galápagos Islands, Darwin studied, among much else, the variances in bird life between the islands. He discovered something very interesting. That there seemed to be a very wide variety of species of Finches. Upon the return of the voyage, Darwin presented his collected specimens to the Zoological Society of London where they were further studied by ornithologist John Gould. It was concluded that the birds were so peculiar that they effectively formed a new group of twelve species. There were other bird specimens collected and it was realised that they seemed to be unique to these islands, even though they closely resembled birds found in South America.

Darwin re-examined the evidence, including specimens collected by FitzRoy himself and concluded that the birds were distinct according to the island that they were found on. From this evidence he developed his ideas on the transmutation of species. Stated simply, these held that, when a particular species was isolated geographically in more than one place, those in different locations would continue to evolve along their own lines. He noticed this particularly with the finches who had evolved different shaped beaks. This was due to the fact that the different islands had variations in the profusion of available nuts. On certain islands, the nuts were larger and harder to crack, which meant that the finches on those islands evolved larger, stronger beaks. Further studies with other species confirmed that similar species separated by geography will evolve differently.

Consequently, Masud considered it understandable that this would also be the case with the human species and that this would explain the genetic differences of the primary human species groups. However, this brought him no closer to understanding the missing link between hominids and Homo sapiens. The various sub divisions of Australopithecus have been dated back to around four million years ago, but these may hardly be thought of as equivalents to Homo sapiens. Indeed, many of these specimens are more akin to apes and the link to us is tenuous at best.

Homo habilis, a controversial species which dates back to just over two million years is perhaps closer and there is evidence that Homo habilis was a tool maker and user. Homo erectus is probably the most likely candidate as examples have been found in the fossil record in Africa, Europe and Asia. Furthermore, those remains discovered to date display a variance in stature with some skeletons being more slender and taller, while some are slightly shorter but noticeably more robust. It is clear that, like many other species, variants of Homo erectus existed in multiple geographic locations and were, like Darwin's finches, developing along slightly different lines. Those discovered so far date from around 1.8 to 0.3 million years ago.

With this evidence, Masud considered that Homo erectus was really the only viable candidate that could be claimed as a direct ancestor to Homo sapiens. There were still considerable differences in skull shape and other features, but there was a pattern being established that would lead onwards towards the very interesting Homo heidelbergensis which, itself, could be considered a species with features from both Homo erectus and Homo sapiens. These fossils have been dated to between 500,000 to 200,000 years ago. This is very interesting as human like fossils have been found around the Mediterranean which date back to around 190,000 years ago and in China which date back to around 120,000 years. It is reasonable to assume that other evidence will be found over time which will help to complete the picture.

And this leads us on to the most fascinating Homo neanderthalensis, remains of which have been found throughout Europe and the Middle East. These range from around 200,000 to around 30,000 years ago and blend directly into the Homo sapiens period. Indeed, it is possible that the two co-existed and equally possible that they interbred. This scenario, together with the aforementioned transmutation of species, might well have led directly to the variations in the human species found throughout the Mesolithic and Neolithic times. This idea, Masud considered entirely feasible. That Homo neanderthalensis had a slightly different cranial shape and a stocky build is little different to the variations found in early Homo sapiens. Indeed, some Anthropologists claim that Homo neanderthalensis was simply another sub-division of Homo sapiens.

But what of modern Homo sapiens and their more recent development? It was clear to Masud that the Mesolithic people were able to follow the retreating ice of the last glaciation and reinhabit areas in both the northern and southern hemispheres which had previously been denied to them. This is clear as evidence has been found of Mesolithic occupation in northern Europe and Scandinavia, among other regions.

And so, this is where Masud's focus fell. The Mesolithic people were, it seems, mostly hunter gatherer's who would roam to mostly familiar locations where they would, occasionally build dwellings which would range from relatively sophisticated designs to some which were probably temporary. This pattern has been found in the Middle East, in Europe, in Canada and elsewhere. From a time-line perspective, many would place the Mesolithic period from about 10,000 years BC to around 4,000 years BC. This was particularly interesting to Masud as he was thinking of those nomadic people who would have first settled along the banks of the Nile and who founded the wonderful world of ancient Egypt. We know a good deal about the Middle Kingdom of ancient Egypt, from around 2040 to 1782 years BC, administered by the Amenemhat and Senruset lines, but rather less about the Old Kingdom, which dates back to around 2575 years BC. However, as Masud understood, precise dating according to our modern methodologies is very difficult when referring to ancient Egypt.

Many considered the Mesolithic peoples as of the classic hunter gatherer persuasion while Neolithic peoples tended to be more settled and cultivated agriculture. However, there is surely an overlap and, in many cultures, the two lifestyles coexisted without conflict. In Canada for example, there were nomadic tribes such as the Plains Cree which often followed the buffalo herds among other activities, but there were also Woodlands Cree who tended to build dwellings, often in more than one place in order that they might migrate from one to the other upon a seasonal basis.

A similar situation surely existed upon the Arabian peninsula and adjacent areas, whereby there were advanced settlements coinciding with the roaming nomadic tribes who continued their lifestyle into the times of the Ottoman occupation of the area. No doubt, the same was true of other areas, whereby people descending directly from those of the Neolithic times would continue to follow the lifestyle of their forbears.

This might well entail regular movement across the land or a more settled approach. The coexistence of such diverse life styles may be found in many areas.

Masud found this consideration of our origins as a species quite fascinating. It was difficult to correlate some of the wilder claims of ape like remains with us as Homo sapiens but, from Homo habilis onward things looked fairly clear cut and Homo erectus surely gave rise to the following variations which would become Homo sapiens. However, upon the tree of life, all of these species are relative latecomers. Many thousands of species had come and gone long before Homo sapiens arrived on the scene. And even then, it was only really since Mesolithic times that we witnessed the very fast development of the human species which then really blossomed during Neolithic times.

Masud further considered that there was an ancient civilisation which was highly advanced at this time and widely distributed. From the Harappan culture of the Indus valley in India, to that of Egypt and Mesopotamia, but with less obvious developments coming along in northern Asia, Europe and Scandinavia. These latter examples were perhaps not as refined, but there seemed to be contact between them nevertheless. This has been shown by archaeological discoveries of ancient tombs in England, for example, which contained trinkets and goods which could have only come from the Far East. We know that, while the Egyptians were master ship wrights and built vessels capable of crossing oceans, so were the Vikings who, undoubtedly crossed the Atlantic Ocean and landed in Canada. The Egyptians, of course, traded throughout the Mediterranean area and, if we think of the Sumerians in the southern part of what we like to call Mesopotamia, it is likely that they also built vessels to enable travel throughout the Persian Gulf. The Sumerians occupied the land which we now like to call Kuwait and, of course, the Kuwaitis have always been renowned as a maritime nation who built vessels of an excellent quality.

Indeed, it seemed to Masud that there were clear lines of development which stretched back to our ancestors who were almost certainly the Homo erectus species. However, the veritable explosion of capability which took place in Neolithic times was most interesting. Nearly everything of value seems to have been derived from those early civilisations, especially those of Egypt, India and Mesopotamia. The ancient Egyptians enjoyed most things which we would consider important today and built some wonderful architecture. Simultaneously, the nomadic tribes continued their roaming but were, in many ways, equally skilled. That they managed to navigate accurately across such vast distances by the stars was truly remarkable and, it seems, they were mostly quite literate and displayed notable skills in the manufacture of garments and other necessities. These people no doubt walked on the same mountains upon which Masud had stood and wondered about them.

They, in turn, may have wondered who trod these paths before they did. Yes, the origins of our species is certainly interesting and Masud started to consider other aspects of what we might call civilisation and, indeed, how we might define humanity.

Language

How did the earliest humans communicate? There is little doubt that they would have done so, just as all animals do, but the development of articulate speech is another matter entirely.

A key development in this context was the ability to stand and walk upright. That Home erectus was bipedal opened up many advantages. One of these was that individuals could more easily make eye contact and, therefore, communicate by facial expression their mood and often their intention toward one another. It is likely that such communication would be accompanied by gesture and the annunciation of sounds, which also would reflect the feelings and, perhaps, the intention of the individual.

Another key development at this time would be the congregation of individuals into social groups. Masud had already discovered that Homo erectus was widely travelled and, even though their total population would have been that of maybe an average sized town today, they were widely dispersed geographically. It seems that groups of individuals wandered off in all directions, probably in search of territory which they could call their own. This activity would automatically be creating distinct social groups and within these groups, individuals would need to be able to identify one another and discriminate among strangers.

Masud considered such factors and it seemed to him that, throughout the predominance of Homo erectus as a distinct species, there were many associated parallel developments which opened up pathways leading to the creation of articulate speech. If, at the beginning of this period, we may imagine a combination of eye contact, facial expression, gesture and a series of distinct sounds associated directly with these gestures, then we are surely on the road towards articulated speech.

Masud found that anthropologists placed much emphasis on the development of brain size and, in particular, the development of certain areas of the brain which supported our cognitive development. There are also areas of the brain and more general neural system which become responsible for the articulation form the tongue and vocal tract. The interesting point here is that all of these factors seemed to be developing in one direction, upon the road towards the capability of articulated speech.

However, even these wonderful developments would not have been enough. There would need to be a steady development of cognitive capability which extended the understanding of the immediate towards imagination and the ability to foresee, or imagine, situations which would be desirable and then to communicate the same to other individuals within the family or wider social group. This may have developed from the previously mentioned combination of direct eye contact, facial expression, gesture and accompanied sound, to a much wider range of sounds and vocalisations, including those which could be heard over large distances. These sounds would be different from those used to communicate affection towards family members, especially when the group was resting.

Consequently, it seems likely that there was an intermediate period along the time line which stretched from early Homo erectus to later Homo sapiens, where social groups would have a collection of distinct sounds with which to communicate not only immediate threats or other real time situations, but to express a desired future situation which would come directly from the imagination of the individual involved. This would be one of the factors that would serve to differentiate Homo erectus and Homo sapiens from the apes.

As Masud considered such matters it occurred to him that these parallel developments in cognitive capability and communication were being undertaken within another evolutionary trend, that of the formation of distinct social groups. Such groups, which we may well call early tribes were likely rivals when it came to territory. Those who had found very supportive locales would want to protect them for their own use. This may explain how many archaeological discoveries have been made in valley areas, close to natural water supplies and good hunting grounds, or in areas where there are abundant materials which may be used in the construction of dwellings, the manufacture of tools or early garments.

This separation of early social groups, or tribes, would of course lead to a distinction within their own developing vocabularies. Different social groups would develop distinct calls and annunciations which would help to identify individuals from the same group. Masud reflected upon how we see this happening very clearly today with birds. Many birds have a wider vocabulary than is at first supposed and, furthermore, they use their distinct, regional vocabularies and dialects in interesting ways. For example, when studying bird song in connection with this work, Masud found that, in the late evening when visual identification was difficult, certain species of birds used calls to perform 'triangulation' in order to pin point and confirm the presence of others within their own group. This may occur across quite substantial distances. Mammals do the same. The beautiful call of the wolf at night is not for no purpose. If one listens carefully, there is always a response, sometimes from quite far away. We are now aware, as Masud mused, that whales do the same thing and that some species of whale can easily communicate over several miles with their powerful vocalisations. In fact, there seem to be few mammals who do not make calls to each other. Many of the apes and smaller monkeys do so, as do wild horses, camels, bears and many other creatures. Masud has already considered bird calls and how these are much more sophisticated than many suppose. Consequently, it is really no surprise that early hominids would have done the same. Homo erectus, within the span of that species, may have developed a sophisticated vocabulary in much the same way and this would have been inherited by early Homo sapiens.

Masud was particularly fascinated by the fact that, at some point, there seemed to be a veritable explosion of human development in early Neolithic times which, no doubt, would have been accompanied by a parallel explosion in communication capability. This enhanced capability would have supported trade and bartering as well as human associations and agreements. Males and females would also be able to find better matches for mating and so further develop the trend.

But of course, as Masud reflected, some of these tribes had now been geographically separated for some considerable time and had grown apart genetically and socially. Their development of a greater articulation and sophistication of speech had progressed along parallel but distinct lines. We were now in the realm of distinct vocabularies or languages, whereby different social groups had developed their own words, their own vocalisations and their own way of putting it all together to create their own special language. In many cases, groups who were closely situated, would develop language with regional similarities making it relatively easy to understand one another at times when they came together. These would have been different dialects but based upon a common foundation. However, as time went by, these distinctions, in some cases, became more acute, making a common understanding more difficult. And, of course, those who wandered far away would develop totally different vocabularies which would not be understood by their contemporaries based elsewhere.

Masud wondered how this same effect manifested itself in the animal world. Birds, who rely much upon sounds and vocalisations, would surely display regional variations, although they were also able to travel vast distances, in the case of migrating birds, and were no doubt exposed to variations which they would come to understand. Masud supposed that it might be harder for mammals and other creatures, but then considered that most animals make full use of their senses when communicating, and would be very well attuned to gestures and body language, among other things.

In any event, spoken language would have undoubtedly played a major part in the flowering of human capabilities which occurred in the Neolithic period. The ability to convey meanings and ideas from one individual to another made it possible to collaborate as a community. To teach and educate others in methods which had been proven. Such a collaboration would make it possible to build robust dwellings, laid out in such a manner as to foster community relations and ready collaboration for the common good. Furthermore it would help to identify particular skills among certain individuals, leading to the creation of defined roles. The next step, of course, would be to develop ways of depicting this language visually in the form of pictures or phonetic scripts. The ancient Egyptians of course developed their system of hieroglyphs which Masud had always considered the most beautiful and logical of all written systems. The Sumerians and others developed various forms of cuneiform and, of course, the Egyptian Coptic script which followed on from the Hieratic and Demotic was a mixture of the latter with Greek and was used to help understand the Egyptian hieroglyphic writing. There were other developments elsewhere in the world but, importantly, this was all leading towards another very important factor.

Skills Development

The ability to write down information in a common language, that others within the same social group or country could read it, meant that instructions could be shared with which to undertake important tasks. In addition, of course, it meant that individuals could communicate with each other without having to be physically in the same space. This was valuable from a number of perspectives. One such use was the ancient Egyptian 'wisdom texts' which could be dictated by the Pharaoh, copied and distributed to all of the main towns where they could be read aloud in public as the Pharaoh's direct words to his people, explaining how they might lead good and happy lives. At the time, this would have been an advanced approach, bearing in mind this was thousands of years before the various 'biblical texts' appeared.

Masud further understood that while writing allowed for important events to be recorded and messages to be sent, there was much more to it than that. It allowed for the communication of ideas across vast distances as well as locally, ensuring that worthwhile developments in any area might be understood and put to use for the common good. Travellers and nomads might observe things in foreign lands that were either innovative or useful in general terms and write down what they saw in order that the knowledge could be brought home and shared. In this respect, writing allowed for a more rapid advance of human ingenuity.

It could also be used for very specific requirements in general administration and governmental affairs. Masud thought of King Hammurabi of Babylon who was a far sighted leader who developed, and had written down, a set of 282 laws for guidance among the general population. This was no minor task as it involved around 4000 lines of text which were not only written on clay tablets but lovingly carved into a diorite stele with an image of the king at its top. There is even a prologue and an epilogue which describe why the laws exist in the first place and how ordinary men might come to the stone stele and read for themselves if there was any doubt as to their meaning. As Masud already understood, diorite is an exceptionally hard stone and is very difficult to carve. But Hammurabi presumably also understood this and that, consequently, his laws would not quickly be eroded. The far sighted king was also setting a pattern for the future of the whole world as the Babylonian legal system was one of the very first to be formally documented. Nowadays, 'law' books are often in collections spanning tens of volumes.

Instructions could also be written down for building work, boat building, the manufacture of tools and musical instruments and much besides. In ancient Egypt, the role of the scribe was a very important one and this would carry forward into later times where, in many countries, literacy was often in the hands of a relative minority, often associated with religion and the creation of religious texts. Alternatively, philosophical works which, indeed, had much in common with religious texts.

Together with the development of the written word came the creation of practical means of calculation for recording values in relation to trade agreements. The ancient Egyptians had long ago developed a decimal system of accounting and the Babylonians developed a fairly complex system which could, if required, manipulate very large numerical values indeed. It was unlikely that they would need anything like this scale of granularity for everyday transactions, but they might well have used the power of their mathematics to calculate values related to natural phenomena. In any event, this ability to calculate and manipulate values in written form was an important development in its own right.

Clearly, the development of articulate speech and the various regional dialects or languages triggered a period of dramatic advance for the human species. Knowledge could now be shared much more widely and more rapidly and language, both spoken and written, allowed for a much closer collaboration within social groups or communities. It was, no doubt, this ready and close collaboration which accelerated the development of all things from agricultural practice, to the manufacture of goods and implements and, of course the most important trade relationships and various trade routes which enabled barter between disparate communities using various numerical systems. It further allowed these communities to liaise together in ways which were not previously possible. The human species had taken a giant leap forwards and this was itself to set the pattern for the future of humanity.

Rivalry

In most species there exists an element of rivalry. This has historically led to the creation of family based tribes, larger communities and, eventually entire disparate nations who, by geographic separation, grow further apart. For trade purposes, as Masud well understood, many of these groups co-operate together and collaborate where it makes sense to do so. Some of them form closer alliances and become friendly nations, at least, up to a point. However, there always exists an element of rivalry, to one degree or another.

Masud wondered how this element of rivalry would first have been introduced to species. His own studies into the natural world had suggested that, initially, species were content to cohabit the beautiful world that they found themselves a part of. When life remained mostly in the warm shallow oceans, characterised by a wealth of anemones and sponge like creatures who derived their nutrients from the sea water itself. With the introduction of the phylum Chordata came the vertebrates and all manner of small fishes. These creatures were mobile and able to more fully exploit the availability of locales rich in nutrients wherein they might best prosper. However, at this stage of evolution there was plenty of space for everyone, especially in the oceans which is where life was developing. There was really no need for rivalry as such although, it is possible that some creatures might become somewhat territorial.

Masud had already understood that a dramatic change was to take place when nature introduced the concept of carbon exchange. There were several quantum leaps forward in natural evolution and this was one of them. With carbon exchange came the separation of predators and prey, with one species preying upon the other with individuals literally consuming each other in order to become stronger and maintain their own metabolism. This, in turn, established the concept of rivalry into the DNA and genetic structure of living beings.

However, as Masud discovered, there was also an interesting dichotomy which developed between those who actively hunted as predators and prey and those who harvested the bounty that nature provided around them. This dichotomy would exist in many phyla, from the anthropods and above, and would eventually manifest itself in Homo erectus and Homo sapiens, where some would be content to harvest the land while others would be hunters of creatures, probably including their own like. In both cases, there may or may not have been territorial issues, perhaps over favoured landscapes but, we must remember, that the total human population would have been extremely low at this time, probably not much more than 10,000 altogether and so there would certainly be enough room for all to find their place and also to roam in search of better hunting grounds. In some cases, this nomadic lifestyle evolved purely because of the animals being hunted, like caribou, buffalo and the like. In other cases a nomadic lifestyle developed both in support of trade, weather patterns and, no doubt, simply because it was an attractive way of living. Simultaneously, in each case, others decided to settle where they were with some having seasonal homes that they would move to at certain times of the year.

This gave rise to people congregating into communities. These would have developed from simple family units, to larger families containing relatives and, eventually, to communities formed in order to collaborate with each other for reasons of both sustenance and security. It would no doubt not be long before these communities were given a distinct name.

Tribes

Once a community had been formed and given a name they would effectively have become a tribe. The steady development of tribes was an important building block for civilisation generally. Masud understood this in particular because, in his own country, many of the inhabitants still considered themselves as being part of, or directly descended from, a distinct tribe. Being a member of a tribe was very important as, if a person was of no particular tribe, they were effectively an outcast and on their own. Being affiliated with a tribe provided the individual with both an identity and a sense of belonging to the greater whole. In addition, it provided security for the individual concerned. There was a great deal of pride associated with being a valuable member of a certain tribe. Inevitably, this would also lead to rivalry between tribes.

The primary issue with rivalry would be that the stronger tribes would consider themselves superior and would prey upon the weaker tribes whom they considered to be inferior. Sometimes these divisions or 'castes' created boundaries that were impossible to cross, often leading to conflict and inter-tribal warfare. We still witness this today and it surely represents a tragedy for the human species as a whole. Throughout history and in many lands there has existed a bitter rivalry between tribes that has, in turn, caused an unspeakable suffering among those caught up in it. This is especially the case for women and children and, of course, the many orphans that are generated as a direct cause of such conflict.

Masud was, in particular, aware of the suffering of so many orphans, regardless of their tribal, political, racial or religious origin. Masud realised that the horrible situation that they found themselves in was not their fault. They were the victims of the prejudice, hatred and rivalry among adults which had left them homeless and without the love and guidance which they all deserved. It seemed to Masud that this was a senseless situation, the worst tragedies of which were often bourn by women and children who had had no part in the rivalry that effectively destroyed their lives. Of course, this rivalry had been in existence ever since humans decided to form tribes. Some of this has a geographical context as, in some countries, tribes had historically coexisted quite well while, in others, they never had done so and probably never will do so, even if there are temporary peace agreements.

Masud then thought about how this gathering of like species worked in the natural world among our brothers and sisters of other kinds. It seemed to him that, while territory was sometimes jealously guarded, there was rarely any conflict born of sheer hatred among most species. Masud thought of the wolves which he had come across in other countries. Yes, they formed family oriented packs which operated as distinct units and an individual from a rival pack would not be welcomed. However, they did not seek conflict and marked their territory in ways which allowed for a truly peaceful coexistence, born from mutual respect. Many birds operated in a similar manner, as did animals which form herds, such as deer and buffalo.

In the animal world, there was sometimes conflict between males seeking mates within the mating season, but this rarely lead to severe violence and was often more about demonstrating prowess to watching females. Indeed, as Masud appreciated, this was simply natural selection taking place in order to ensure the ongoing wellbeing of the group as a whole. The more successful males passing on their genetic inheritance to the next generation. This was simply a facet of nature which was integral to the processes of evolution.

But humans are different. Or at least, they have become different as a result of what Masud often referred to as the 'greed culture'. Among modern humans, success is not measured by accomplishment, hounourability, decency, kindness, understanding or humanity. No, it is measured by wealth and by perceived position or power over others within the community. The unfortunate reality, as Masud had seen in many countries, is that children are conditioned to equate success in life purely with how much money they can make. Anything else has become meaningless to most of the modern world.

Masud reflected much upon this situation. Was he exaggerating this characteristic? he looked around him and thought of the many places he had travelled to. Wealthy men were looked up to while the poor were despised. Those who achieved shallow and false celebrity either via the media or, perhaps, because of sports activities or popular culture entertainment, were similarly revered and worshipped. Masud then thought about the many who were helping others, undertaking charitable works, but in obscurity and those who had made solid contributions to our knowledge in the natural and physical sciences, all of whom would never be acknowledged or thanked in any way for their valuable contribution as human beings. Of course, this was not why they were undertaking such works but, nevertheless, there were surely many such people within every society in every land. There was no official recognition for them. No hero worship. No exaggerated financial reward. There formed a silent minority who shunned celebrity and recognition. If they had been born a member of a particular tribe or caste, it made no difference to them. They were of those who were on the straight path and would not be deflected by either financial gain or public recognition.

Masud had thought much about this. It weighed upon his mind that there were so many hypocrites in the modern world and so many grasping, nasty people who would stop at nothing to achieve their unworthy ambitions. He realised how lucky he had been to be born into a good family with a learned and kind father at the head who had passed down his own wisdom and understanding to Masud. Similarly, his dear Aaliyah was the sweetest of persons who also showed much kindness, understanding and tenderness towards others. Masud would not have changed his life for any other, regardless of any attached wealth or power. He had realised what really matters in this world.

Travel

Ever since Homo erectus and the later Homo sapiens had appeared, it seems that they enjoyed travelling. Indeed, for many, this nomadic way of life would continue on for thousands of years and, in some remote regions, it still occurs today. Masud had understood this well and could see the attractions of such a lifestyle even though settlements were the norm today.

However, it seems that this nomadic life style was firmly established in the Mesolithic period, sometimes known as the Middle Stone Age, between around 8000 BC to 2700 BC when the Neolithic took over. Mesolithic human remains and traces of human activity have been found almost everywhere. It is perhaps understandable that Mesolithic humans would have wandered in East Africa, India, on the Arabian peninsula and further north. But they were also in the northern lands, in Scandinavia, Russia and throughout Europe. Even on some of the small, remote islands within the British Isles, Mesolithic remains have been found. Masud wondered how on Earth did they get there? Some of these small islands are visible from the mainland on a clear day, some not. In any event, it occurred to Masud, that they would have had to construct some rudimentary vessel in order to make the crossing, or did they? Is it possible that they simply swam across? It would certainly have been possible for those in good health, maybe adventurous youngsters.

This ability and fondness for travel seemed to be ingrained in early humans. To some extent, if they were foraging, then it is expected that they would wander, at least within their home vicinity. However, bearing in mind that most places were much more thickly forested than today it is unlikely that they would need to travel far in order to find food. For hunter gatherers there would have been a rich source of food almost everywhere. They needed to have access to water of course and this fact might have held a tendency to settle in advantages spots, but no, they continued to wander. And they covered vast distances, on foot and through all sorts of terrain, much of it forested.

Masud mused about these early people and wondered what motivated them most about life. No doubt they would have looked up at the stars and noted the journeying of the sun and moon. Perhaps these were among the first natural objects that they found names for. They would have understood the rain coming down from dark clouds, and been thankful for it. Indeed, they probably would have had an understanding of the natural cycles that would be close to our scientific understanding today, maybe not in precise detail, but certainly conceptually. They would also have studied the movements of the game that they hunted and would probably quickly get a feel for where the herds would be at certain times of the year. This would have likely led to a certain amount of seasonal travel, but not to the great journeys which these early people clearly undertook. Would they have named specific places? Almost certainly, even as the rudimentaries of speech slowly unfolded and evolved.

It seems then that some families and tribes would have roamed in distinct patterns within a given area, based upon the seasonal availability of foodstuffs and water. And yet, others it seems, simply roamed and kept on roaming. Exploring the world which they found themselves within and, no doubt, excited to discover new lands and territories which, perhaps, held a different variety of species. Even so, some of these remote islands where Mesolithic remains have been found were desolate places where, one would imagine, no one would particularly wish to stay. Was it perhaps this very remoteness that was attractive to those who occupied these places? Was there an aesthetic? An appreciation of the wild and beautiful?

In any event, early humans, who had already mastered the making of basic tools, were widely travelled in both hemispheres, but particularly in the north. They roamed almost everywhere and obviously enjoyed this freedom of movement which their early lifestyle permitted. A luxury which we do not enjoy today. One wonders also at their ability to navigate. They must surely have been able to navigate to favourite places which were already known to them and, it is highly likely given later developments, that they would have used the heavenly bodies as their reference points, along with distinct geographic features. This would also be a time where early trails were being forged that others might follow in the wake of pioneers.

Transportation

Masud was intrigued to think about the first use of transportation. It is likely that donkeys and mules may have been used initially as these creatures where quite easy to capture and to domesticate. They would have been very useful for carrying loads between one place and another. Quite possibly, this is how the first caravans or 'mule trains' appeared. Whether or not humans immediately thought of riding on them themselves is hard to say. Possibly, they might have been used to help carry the frail or sick and this use would no doubt have occurred to them.

But then there was another huge leap forward within the realms of human travel. The domestication of the horse. Horses would have been seen and no doubt admired from very early times. They were thought to have been domesticated around 3500 BC on the steppes of southern Russia and Kazakhstan and then, in the Near East, at around 2300 BC. There was a special and quite magical relationship which quickly formed between man and horse. The horse was not simply a beast of burden and, from the earliest times, good horses were highly prized and would have been well cared for. Indeed, this would develop into something approaching an obsession during the Neolithic period, especially throughout the Middle East. From around 2000 BC onwards, a variety of chariots and carts were in regular use and, as we can see from what we know of ancient Egypt, some of these chariots were exquisite creations. No doubt they were in evidence across Sinai and throughout the peninsula.

This use of the horse would have allowed wider travel and, importantly, faster travel. This latter factor greatly benefited the Mongolians under Genghis Khan 1162-1227 whose empire spread rapidly and decisively throughout much of the world. The Mongols were (and remain) superb horsemen with riding skills that far surpassed their rivals. Even today, in Mongolia, Masud discovered that there are more horses than people and they remain highly prized. They also survive in the wild in temperatures from -40° C to +30° C and are slightly smaller in stature than other breeds. Furthermore, equine events still have a prominent place in the broader Mongolian activities.

And so, the horse has always played an important part in travel and has been a close companion of man in many areas from commerce to warfare. Indeed, the horse has shared the calamities of warfare with man, often disastrously so, as was the case during the Great War when countless numbers of them perished alongside their human comrades. The tragedy is that it was humans who were responsible for leading them into this carnage and, no doubt, many humans felt this all too keenly. After all, the relationship between horse and man was often a very personal one. In each case, the one never forgetting the other.

There was of course another quadruped who equally bonded with humans and became a very important part of their lives with respect to travel. The ship of the desert. The camel. Many consider camels to be of superior intelligence to the horse. They are certainly different in character and it is well documented that camels have long memories, identify both each other and their human companions with ease and, in many cases have a very distinct personality.

Masud found it difficult to accurately define the date of the introduction of the camel for human transportation needs. Some would hold that this was around 5000 BC, some that it was much later, probably around 2000 BC and on the Arabian peninsula. However camels, like humans, were present in many areas and it is likely that they were used from north Africa, across the peninsula and to India and back. Possibly their initial usage was simply among families, both for carrying loads and for their milk. No doubt it was quickly realised that camels displayed noteworthy endurance and could walk for many miles carrying loads and with the minimum of water. This single feat rendered them invaluable for humans as they could now undertake journeys which would have been unthinkable without the camel. This factor is, of course, what led to the creation of the various trade routes which stretched for enormous distances. The Silk Road, yes, but there were other examples and the nomadic tribes, with the help of their camel friends could travel from north Africa and Egypt, across the peninsula to the Persian Gulf, up and across to northern India and down to present day Oman, Yemen and the Indian Ocean as well as throughout the Holy Land and up to present day Syria. Indeed, there was nowhere the nomad could not go with his camel caravan, stopping as necessary along the way to pitch camp for a while and maybe meet with others.

The camel, being such an essential for this purpose, was highly prized and generally well cared for. As Lawrence discovered during the Great War, there were also racing camels and highly thought of individual camels were known, often by name, across the nomadic tribes. Indeed, his own favourite, Gazala, was one such camel who enjoyed a welcome wherever she went. The camel is superbly adapted for life in the desert. She can open and close her nostrils at will, in the event of sand storms or strong winds and the entire respiratory system is designed to regulate the temperature of both incoming and outgoing air, condensing this to water when necessary. Masud realised that the camel was yet another miracle of nature whose design was inexplicable. Camels themselves have evolved some interesting behavioural patterns which display an uncommon level of understanding. Among these is the way they will lay down, either individually or in groups. They are adept and positioning themselves in such a manner that the least possible surface area is exposed directly to the sun. Often this means facing the sun directly, which might seem odd to us at first but which actually makes perfect sense. When in a group, they will usually huddle together which, again, would seem counter-intuitive to us but which also makes good sense as the group as a whole exposes less surface area to the sun. As Masud mused, the camel was indeed a gift to human kind.

And so things might have continued except, the design of the internal combustion engine and its application to what had previously been horse drawn buggies, changed everything and in a very significant manner. No doubt many wonder, with hindsight, whether this was really such a good thing. It certainly facilitated the building of countless roads but, of course, we already had the best road of all, the rail road. Steam locomotives had brought longer distance travel to the masses and many were enjoying this new found freedom of movement as the Industrial Revolution unfolded. In some countries there was a healthy competition among different service providers, in others, the railways were state owned and well operated. In one country however, a very unfair monopoly was created by one family who became enormously wealthy as a result. This is mentioned because, as Masud's research had shown, this was, indirectly, to play a very significant part in the second World War, together with other, connected, monopolies from the same country. We had come a very long way from working with horses and camels.

Then came air travel and even space travel. Much speculation evolves around the latter, accompanied with a good deal of marketing propaganda and some very dishonest business practices. Air transportation has had an interesting history however and, of course, air power plays a significant part in modern warfare.

In conclusion, travel and transportation have played a very significant part in human development. Indeed, as Masud mused, they have played an equally significant part in the evolution of humanity. Some would hold that this has not always been positive. However, there it is.

Weaponry

From Mesolithic times onward, humans had discovered that they could make weapons with which to help them hunt. Rudimentary spears and later arrow heads have been found in reasonable numbers all over the world. This was all part and parcel of the tool making skills that early Stone Age peoples displayed. At first, these would have simply been carefully selected stones used for scraping skins and other such activities, before it was discovered that such tools could be fashioned as desired, with a little imagination. This lead to the creation of spears, used to hunt game and while these have been commonly associated with Mesolithic times and later, Masud has found that modern research is changing this opinion.

It is now considered that humans were fashioning crude spears in the Middle Pleistocene, a period associated with Homo heidelbergensis, thought to be the last common ancestor of the Neanderthals who were, in turn, coexistent with Homo sapiens. These artifacts are thought to stretch back almost 300,000 years. If this is the case, this would indeed be quite remarkable as it would demonstrate a coordinated reasoning among very early humans, as well as cooperation with regard to hunting. After all, it would be unlikely that one or two individuals would think of this in isolation. More probably, one group experimented with the idea and then passed this knowledge on to others who copied their example.

Masud found that dating the first use of the bow and arrow was more problematic. Some sources suggest that arrow tips made of bone have been found in South Africa which date back almost 60,000 years. However, such claims are rather tenuous. It is more likely that the bow and arrow also dates back to Mesolithic times and, indeed, the bow thought to be the oldest surviving relic of the type was found in peat bogs on an island near Denmark (referred to as the Holmegaard bow) which is around 10,000 years old. While arrow heads have been found in Germany and elsewhere which are slightly older, no older bow has been discovered.

The use of the bow and arrow was perhaps perfected on the Eurasian Steppes and later in and around the Mediterranean. In later times, it was used around the world and the Mongol horsemen in particular became adept and using the bow while mounted on horseback. And, of course, the bow was in common use in ancient Egypt and no doubt throughout Mesopotamia.

What would have varied quite considerably would no doubt be the skill of those making the arrows and fixing the tips to them. From bone to stone to iron, these arrow heads were almost an art form in themselves and a skilled arrow maker, later called a Fletcher, would have been a valued asset in any tribe or grouping of individuals. The sheer number of such arrows being made, even in those early times, would have been prodigious. By the time we reach the Medieval period, they would have been manufactured in their thousands. In Tudor times, the English perfected the Long Bow, which gave them an advantage in open warfare as the Long Bow propelled beautifully prepared arrows with a velocity and force previously unknown.

In many cultures and many geographic areas around the world, the bow and arrow became the primary weapon, firstly for hunting game and eventually, for warfare between tribes or nations. Consequently, the skilled use of a bow was a desirable attribute for any man in any culture.

In China, somewhere around the 10th or 11th century, it is clear that tubes were used to shoot projectiles by the use of gunpowder. These evolved from simple lance mounted tubes to canon like devices which appeared in the 12th and 13th centuries. These would have quickly been noticed by those trading with China or otherwise coming into contact with them and it would not be long before the use of gunpowder would spread around the known world, together with the idea of launching a ball or other projectile from a device powered by gunpowder. Initially such devices would have been mostly canon, either drawn on sledges or eventually mounted upon purpose built carraiges. These carraiges would themselves quickly evolve into what were commonly known as 'gun carriages' which would be designed as two parts. When being transported, the two parts would be coupled together and drawn by horses. When in use, the two parts would be split to enable the canon to be more steadfastly connected to the ground from where it could be aimed more accurately. A variation of this approach would eventually be used on board ships where, mounted upon much smaller wheels, the canon could be slid back and forth for muzzle loading and pointing back out through the gun ports on the ship.

It would be logical enough to question whether a similar approach could be applied to a hand held device. If it could, then it might make the use of bows less relevant and such a device might be more easily carried. The Chinese had certainly made portable devices, of a kind, but the familiar flintlock pistol was produced in Europe in the 16th century. These were muzzle loading designs which fired a single ball, albeit after a good deal of preparation. They could be made to be reasonably accurate, at least in skilled hands, and were quite powerful. It was not long before the practice of duelling with pistols became commonplace where, previously, swords or rapiers would have been used.

The flint lock firing mechanism could be temperamental and, in the 1820s, a new methodology arrived in the form of a percussion cap. Used in combination with the charge to be fired, the percussion cap enabled the pistol to be used in all weathers and also brought new levels of reliability to the use of hand guns. Perhaps, for the first time, they were reliable enough to be used as a weapon in open conflict. The next step, which must have seemed obvious to some, was to combine the percussion element with the charge into a single bullet. From here, it was a short step to the design of the revolver in the early 19th century and then on to various automatic hand guns which held a slide of bullets, usually situated in the grip.

Of course, throughout this development of the handgun, similar progress was being made in rifles. From musket loading devices firing balls to single shot percussive devices and on to bullets and then rifles with clips of bullets to be used in the field. The particularly deadly machine gun which would be capable of sustained rapid fire of between 500-1000 shots per minute, fed by a belt of ammunition. These horrible weapons were developed in the late 19th century and were used to devastating effect during The Great War.

Whilst guns of all types had always been used in human conflict, as well as to shoot game. The machine gun was designed solely for human conflict and to be able to kill as many humans as possible in the shortest possible time. It was and remains one of the most horrible inventions of human ingenuity. Those using them ceased to be humans and became degraded into being mere killing machines. Masud reflected that the same is true today. The other equally evil invention used for similar purposes was the flame thrower which, no doubt, some would argue could be used to destroy buildings or stores, in reality, it has most often been used simply to kill people. Such weapons are simply the manifestation of evil. In recent times, the accuracy and range which both may be used over has increased.

Alongside these developments of all manner of weaponry there have been parallel developments of the base from which such things might be used. Originally, this may have been primarily ships although, from an individual perspective, many tribes and cultures became adept at firing guns from horseback, some of them maintaining this as a proud tradition.

Far worse, was the development of tanks, purpose built all terrain vehicles from which both heavy canon and machine guns might be fired without exposing their occupants to too much danger. Ships, of course, became much larger until they were huge battleships with hundreds of crew members. The latter of these developments though proved to be especially deadly and that was firing from aircraft. While early aircraft might have mostly fought each other, it would not be long before unscrupulous nations began to fire upon those on the ground, including civilians. From here, it was a short step to dropping bombs and then on to purpose built bombers which could drop heavy loads upon both military and civilian targets. The second World War saw extensive use of bomber aircraft which wreaked huge damage upon mostly civilian targets and were used to terrorise populations. This was another development which may surely be described as evil. However, the evil has not stopped there and we now have smaller aircraft capable of firing rockets with great accuracy into whatever targets they choose. Masud has been both shocked and ashamed to see this tactic being used repeatedly in the Middle East while the so called civilised world does nothing to stop this particular evil.

Aggression

And so, the concept of weaponry was originally conceived as an efficient manner with which to hunt game. However, given the complexities of human nature, it would not be too long before humans turned upon each other using the same implements. This, of course, created an effective 'arms race' whereupon each development would be replaced with an even deadlier one. The practice continues today and, after the Americans reneged on their promise to use nuclear weapons merely as a threat and bombed both Hiroshima and Nagasaki in August 1945, there is the constant possibility that someone may do this again. The attacks on Japan murdered over 200,000 civilians, many of them dying in agony from burns. The war was virtually over at this time anyway so the claims that these attacks ended the war were exaggerated. This, as Masud reflected, was simply another manifestation of evil. Now, it is likely that several world powers have a nuclear capability of one sort or another and this is often used as a thinly veiled threat. Even though many humanitarian organisations continue to point out the absurdity of this as well as the possible consequences of a tit for tat nuclear attack sequence, still, nuclear weapons development undoubtedly continues within many nations. Others have a nuclear capability used for power generation, but the principles are similar and, if deemed necessary, these nations could easily develop nuclear weaponry.

Some maintain that there will never be a nuclear war because everyone concerned understands the probable consequences. Masud considers this a tenuous stance at best as we have already observed throughout history so many cases of aggression and oppression from the strong to the weak and for no particular reason except to steal resources and land. Indeed, we are seeing this today in certain areas and while nuclear weaponry has not been used, weapons of major destruction have been used extensively against civilians, even deliberately targeting refugee camps, mostly populated with women and children. Anyone who can commit such crimes against humanity is assuredly evil. What is worse, as Masud understands only too well, this evil is tolerated and condoned by the so called 'civilised' nations of the world.

The provision of weaponry therefore has been a major development within the broader evolution of the human species. It has served to alter our personalities and our view of each other and, as some may hold, has brought out the very worst of the human psyche. The really big question now is how will these developments continue and what form will they take, as the population of the world continues to expand exponentially and as basic resources necessary to sustain life remain finite. It is a question which needs to be carefully considered in order that more sustainable plans may be developed for the future of human kind in general. Masud is aware that the behaviour of world powers at present does not seem to acknowledge this reality. Weaponry may yet be used in ways even more evil than has hitherto been the case. It is one of the less attractive facets of humanity.

Trade

From the time when most Homo Sapiens were hunter gatherers, it would have no doubt occurred to some of them to trade with each other. Probably this would have initially taken the form of trading valued natural objects such as rocks and minerals which had been discovered in their wanderings. There is substantial evidence of this to be found at various ancient burial sites where, especially in the case of those of apparent high social standing, many personal artifacts have been found including a variety of beads, precious stones and a mixture of valued personal belongings.

It is interesting that this burial of personal items with the body of the individual took place in many cultures. After all, such valued items could easily have been simply distributed among relatives or others within the community, but were instead kept with their original owner. Early humans would have course realised that the spirit or life force had left the body, but would nevertheless had considered that such personal items should remain with the original owner. Perhaps this stemmed from a belief in the afterlife and that, somehow, the individual would still be able to use these items or that they would otherwise bring them pleasure. At various stages of the ancient Egyptian culture, a cross section of items including foodstuffs would often be buried with the individual, that they might be sustained in the afterlife.

In any event, the concept of aesthetics and that certain objects and natural elements were highly prized among individuals, took route at a very early stage of human development. As skills increased and humans started to manufacture objects for use in their everyday lives, those which were of a particularly high quality or prized for their aesthetic appearance, would be valued both by the host community and others whom they happened to meet in the course of their wanderings. Whenever two or more tribes did come together, it would seem natural that they would show each other their particular range of manufactured items and, of course, there would be differences based on the very particular skills or requirements of each tribe. Such differences would no doubt be a source of discussion and perhaps admiration leading to the idea of exchanging, or trading, one such item for another.

Before too long, this concept of trading would become an expected and important part of any meeting between two or more social groups. This idea would grow during the stone age and bronze age and continue throughout most of the ancient cultures. No doubt it was not long before the idea of simply stealing that which was considered of value would occur to various tribes and social groups and the idea of undertaking raids for that purpose would also grew. Masud considered that this development represented a fundamental flaw in human nature and, of course, some communities and even nations became adept at the practice. Sometimes this would simply be between tribes occupying the same land or country and sometimes it would be a persistent activity between countries or larger social communities. In ancient Egypt, a small army was maintained, mainly to protect the country from raids by the Hittites in the north and also from various tribes in the south which we might now call the Somalis. In Scandinavia, the Vikings, who had learned to build ocean going vessels, took the idea even further and used these vessels to undertake raids upon the British isles and northern Europe in particular.

However, there was another side to both trading and the undertaking of raids upon foreign territories, which was somewhat less appealing. This was the trade in human beings. This may have started with the trade of young women to be taken as wives by those undertaking the transaction, a practice which continued into modern times. However, this developed into simply the trading of individuals, to be used however the other party wished and this of course would become the slave trade that reverberated around most of the known world. It was often complemented by the fact that those taken in battle would also be taken as slaves. This was surely one of the most unpleasant factors of the human psyche and yet the practice continues to this day. Masud found that in several cultures, young girls from as little as twelve years of age are sold to others as 'brides' although they may well find themselves in an altogether different situation including, far too frequently, enforced prostitution. This practice is much more prevalent in the modern world than many would believe. It occurs in the Middle East, on the African and Indian continents and, in Canada, the problem of First Nation girls being abducted from the reserved lands and taken into the cities where they are forced into prostitution, remains alarmingly prevalent. What is worse, is that a great many of these girls, when considered of no further use, or if they will not cooperate, are simply murdered, the cause of death usually being given as 'BIT' or blunt instrument trauma. In other words, they are beaten to death. Every year, many of them meet this fate. Similar things happen in the other areas mentioned.

Another form of human trading or slavery is the migrant trail which runs from middle Africa, through the Mediterranean area and into Europe, with other routes coming from Asia. Having paid, often everything they have, to these traders, they find themselves effectively working as slaves in underground factories and other such positions. There are variations on this theme which, no doubt, occur in the Americas and elsewhere. The underlying problem which makes this modern form of human trading possible is the dramatic rise in human population which, in some areas, is simply not sustainable and so, many hundreds of thousands of people living in poverty want to move to somewhere else. Of course, this will create similar problems in the areas that they move to and this opens the door for the evildoers to undertake their trade.

For thousands of years there has been trading in a variety of commodities, including fruit, spices, vegetables, minerals and, more latterly, fuel of various kinds. This was complemented by the trade of manufactured goods which ran parallel. Such trading continues of course today, however, it is not always considered as fair trading. There are many monopolies in place and the few who maintain these monopolies become super wealthy at the expense of others. Unfortunately, we are seeing this everywhere and it is a continuing practice. In some industries there are just a small handful of suppliers who have become huge mostly through restrictive practice which should never have been allowed. This is an unattractive form of trading which, unfortunately, has become the norm and which shows no sign of ceasing.

This idea of restrictive practice and unfair competition was embedded with a vengeance just after the second World War by a particular country whose goal it was to do so and to effectively take over the world, at least in all of the primary market areas. It achieves this often by deliberately destabilising a targeted industry, causing chaos and then moving in with its own version of the same thing, but in a very restrictive manner which disallows any genuine competition. It does this country by country and it is perhaps somewhat alarming that most have not noticed this and simply accept what is happening as though it was normal, acceptable practice.

And so, trade takes various forms and from mostly fair beginnings of mutually beneficial exchange, has further developed over the years into a predatory instrument with which to dominate and control communities and nations alike. This is almost akin to psychological warfare as such trade has an undue influence upon the targeted consumers. At a higher level, countries may enter into trade agreements which, typically, benefit a few at the expense of the many.

Calculation

Even before the advent of monetary systems, it was important to calculate the relative values of goods, produce and associated services. Different items might be calculated directly according to their perceived value against others or work performed. For example, a pot may be exchanged for five loaves of bread. A bag of spices exchanged for some vegetables. Or an amount of grain given for five days work and so on. In other words values of goods and services needed to be defined and agreed. When individuals were trading together, they might simply agree upon what these values were on a transaction by transaction basis. However, when the trade was effectively between the state and the individual, then a clear description of values and amounts given in exchange for work of various kinds would need to be drawn up and agreed upon. State administrators would then be responsible for ensuring that workers were paid according to these agreed rates. For example, in ancient Egypt, at certain times, manual workers and craftsmen were paid in allowances of grain and beer.

These sorts of agreements would have formed the backbone of trade across the ancient world until it was decided that an intermediate value item could be used for calculating the worth of any item. This would be used simply in calculation and recording. The tally may or may not be represented as a physical token, but the accounting for an exchange of some sort would be recorded using written systems and clay tablets among other things. The ancient Egyptians, Babylonians, Sumerians and others used this sort of system for some time. The astonishing thing was the granularity of their calculations and the ability to calculate very large numbers which could not possibly be used for mere bartering of goods and services. Babylonian and Sumerian mathematics were, in fact, highly advanced in the Neolithic period and the use of Cuneiform for such purposes was far more sophisticated than the modern world once believed. The ancient Egyptians used a decimal system which could also serve to represent very high numbers indeed. There is evidence emerging that both India and China seemed to practice accounting in a not dissimilar manner. This sort of accounting was indeed used in the area of trade, but surely was much more widely used as a methodology for measurement in general. For example, the ancient Egyptians measured the height of the Nile river every year. Distances between places would be measured and, of course, the calculations required for the construction of some of the temple complexes and monumental works would have been especially detailed and granular. Consequently, it was obvious that the ancient Egyptians in particular had a complete understanding of geometry and, no doubt, what we would call trigonometry. These skills would also be used in the building of ocean going vessels which was undertaken in many areas from Egypt to the Persian Gulf.

The jump from this type of calculation of values to the advent of currency and coinage is one which it is hard to be precise about. It seems that the Chinese had something of a coining mint in operation around 600 years BC. Of course, the Romans introduced coins around 300 years BC and these were offered in a variety of styles and often bearing the portrait of the emperor of the day. The denarius being a popular example which inspired many other currency systems. Due to the extent of the Roman empire, these coins spread rapidly and were used extensively across a wide geographic area. The idea of coining mints was also introduced and the Romans established many such mints throughout the empire, ensuring that any new design of coin could quickly be implemented and introduced into a wide circulation. Thus, the Roman coinage could also be used for propaganda purposes and to ensure that everyone knew who the current emperor was. Roman coins were issued in gold, silver, bronze and copper and this also set a precedent for others to follow.

However, the problem with using valuable metals such as gold and silver was that the coins could be cropped slightly, with small amounts of gold or silver removed. If an unscrupulous individual did this to a sufficient number of coins, they could of course amass a valuable amount of the precious metal for themselves. This could then be melted down into some other shape, such as a gold bar, and sold at a high profit. This was happening all the time and for many, the financial gain outweighed the risk of being caught. However, in England, Isaac Newton was put in charge of the Royal Mint in 1696 and, under his guidance, methodologies and production techniques were introduced, including the milled edging of coins, to defeat the fraudsters. One visitor to England who noticed this was Peter the Great from Russia. Peter had come to England to learn about ship building as he wanted Russia to have its own navy. By chance he met with Isaac Newton and the two men became friends. This seemed a most unlikely alliance as it was well known that Isaac Newton did not make friends easily and had a reputation as a rather prickly character. Nevertheless, the two men enjoyed going around London together and, when Peter saw what

Isaac Newton had achieved with the Royal Mint, he was very impressed and invited Isaac back to Russia. It was also well known that Isaac Newton disliked travel. Even between Cambridge and London. And yet, surprisingly, he agreed and did indeed travel with Peter back to Russia where he helped him to establish a Russian Mint along similar lines. Today, Isaac is fondly remembered at the Russian Mint museum in St. Petersburg.

Of course, a big change in trade was the introduction of the bank note. As Masud discovered, if we think of a bank note as an agreement to pay a specified amount either on demand or according to a schedule, then we can trace its development back to Hammurabi codes at 1755 to 1750 BC. However, bank notes which would look more familiar to us now as agreements to pay the bearer on demand a certain sum, may be traced back to around 1695 in England, when the Bank of England issued such notes to help finance the wars with France. Sweden did in fact issue a bank note in 1661, but this led to a failure of Stockholms Banco due to over issue and an inability to honour the notes.

Nevertheless, the idea of bank notes was quickly taken up around the world and many Government printing facilities established accordingly. One issue which arose was the suspicion of some countries simply printing money when they did not have the funds to support it. This often led to rapid inflation and innocent people suffering financial loss. Today, there is a much larger problem looming on the horizon and that is the sceptre of the cashless society. This is surely a tragedy just waiting to happen as increasing numbers of retailers and other organisations no longer take cash and rely on either debit cards or mobile phones in order to make what is effectively an online transaction. Placing such a dependency upon third party networks is surely a very bad thing to do, especially when these networks and their supposed security are in the hands of just a few giant organisations. This was proven in recent times with an almost global shutdown of systems which affected banks, airlines, hospitals and, in fact, everyone who depended on such an unintelligent way of managing transactions of any kind.

When global trade, from massive Government and corporate transactions to private transactions, relies solely upon computers and computer networks, we may expect serious problems which are surely against the interest of ordinary decent citizens. But this is exactly what is happening. The mass closure of physical banks in Britain and Europe has also been absolutely against the common interest but the banks have effectively reneged on their promise to users and have prevented ordinary people from having ready access to their own money. This may be considered as a form of fraud, sanctioned by Government, as nearly all banks did this simultaneously in order to force their customers to use online services and, of course, make large numbers of staff redundant. This grossly irresponsible act will have affected countless thousands of small traders who would ordinarily have used their local bank. Now, they may find a branch many tens of miles away, if they are lucky, but this means taking time out of their business activities. Consequently, they will also try to force their own customers to pay electronically which, as we have seen, places everyone at risk.

Countries need trade, at all levels, in order to thrive and remain viable. If such trading transactions rely upon a network established and run by just one or two giant organisations, then the whole thing is both open to both fraud and operational failure, both of which are outside the control of ordinary citizens. This is a very bad development for local, national and international trade and is, in fact, a very bad development for humanity.

The other factor in calculation and exchange was of course the calculation machine. Such machines were introduced in order to remove human error from arithmetic calculations. In 1642, Blaise Pascal developed a machine which would help people, like his father who was a tax official, to undertake repetitive calculations without error. After a number of revisions he finally presented it to the public gaze in 1645, dedicating it to Pierre Seguier, the French Chancellor. It seems however that Pascal was not the first to build such a machine as Wilhelm Schickard had done so back in 1623, although this does not appear to have gained much success. And then, in 1672, Gottfried Leibniz designed a machine known as the 'stepped reckoner' using a rotating drum device which he called the

Leibniz wheel. There were, no doubt, several others experimenting with such devices at this time in both Europe and elsewhere. The idea of machines which could perform calculations was, after all, an attractive one. Over the next two hundred years, many designs of calculating machines were introduced, all of which were designed for relatively straightforward operations.

Then, in 1823, the Englishman Charles Babbage finally gained Government support to build his 'Difference Engine'. This was the forerunner of the digital computer which could solve almost any sort of problem and which had a 20 decimal capacity. This represented a quite extraordinary leap in terms of technology. But then, Charles Babbage was an extraordinary man. A polymath genius with interests in all of the accepted sciences as well as some which were not fully developed. Like many unusually gifted individuals, Babbage was not known for diplomacy and would have difficulty explaining his ideas to laymen and even other scientists. However, an unlikely ally appeared in the form of Ada Lovelace who was, herself, a gifted mathematician who would quickly understand the essence of Babbage's work and became a loyal supporter. By the mid 1830s Babbage had developed further plans for his 'Analytic Engine' which was even more advanced. It may be difficult for some today to appreciate the significance of the work of this eccentric genius. Babbage's engines were fully capable digital computers, operated by cranking handles, which could calculate almost anything. They even included the ability to print out the results. Indeed, this was a key factor of their design as Babbage had noticed errors in books of logarithmic tables and this had inspired him to build something which could calculate huge values and then print out the results.

Unfortunately, Babbage never saw his extraordinary designs in operation, as construction in those days was beyond the capabilities of most engineers. For the next two hundred years or so, scientists debated whether his designs as drawn would actually work and then, in 1991, the bicentennial year of Babbage's birth, the Science Museum in London actually built a difference engine. It was a huge project and when completed, of course, it worked perfectly. By 2002, they had added the printing mechanism, as designed by Babbage, which also worked flawlessly.

And so, trade, currency and calculation are inter linked throughout history in sometimes surprising ways. Indeed, humans have been most ingenious in the development of such things but not always for the common good. In more recent times, predatory and restrictive practices have made things worse in nearly every respect and the current incessant drive towards a cashless society will undoubtedly prove a disaster for ordinary citizens, although it will be portrayed as a benefit.

Nature

When considering humanity and its progression from Homo Erectus to the modern era, it is easy to forget the importance of the natural world and all that it has given us. This was far better understood by ancient civilisations who simply had to work closely with nature and get to understand how the natural world worked. After all, it was the natural world who provided them with everything they needed, from food to rudimentary clothes and, of course, building materials.

The latter seems to have been grasped early on, even in the Mesolithic period when so called 'hunter gatherers' would often wander between known places, either following herds of wildlife or simply as a matter of routine. Anything from makeshift shelters to impressive looking camps would be constructed throughout this period. By Neolithic times, things had changed dramatically with very advanced building projects being undertaken in the Indus Valley, the Nile Valley and across the Arabian peninsula, among other sites in the world. They varied in their complexity and scale, but the die had been set and humans were leaving their mark upon the land as they had never done before. The truly wondrous thing here is that some of these early settlements were built upon islands that were, and remain, very difficult to get to, let alone build upon. Sometimes, this desire for remoteness was to avoid religious or cultural persecution, but not always. It seems that early humans simply had a love affair with nature and chose to be close to it. This was a factor which Masud understood absolutely. He was never happier than when wandering alone in the mountains or across the desert.

Today, many who are lucky enough to be able to travel, do so to sites of natural beauty. The mountains, the sea, forests and lakes and so on. We have a natural affinity with the natural world which, for many individuals, cannot be denied. Some of the scenes which we gaze upon lovingly today, our ancestors gazed upon many thousands of years ago, even though much has changed since that time.

But what exactly do we mean by the word 'nature'? To many it simply means wild, unspoiled places which have not been altered too much by man. To others, it is more concerned with the animal world and all its myriad variations which are so miraculous. It is hard to contemplate nature without acknowledging that there simply must be a higher intelligence which is responsible for all of these wondrous natural creations. In some cultures, this higher intelligence is simply referred to as The Great Spirit. In others it is God. In many it is Allah. However, the Holy Quran tells us that Allah may not be visualised or conceptualised by us. He is an omnipresent spirit, responsible for all that is in the Heavens, on Earth and everything between. This idea is consistent with the view of many philosophers, both in the ancient world and later, who had absolute faith in this higher intelligence which is responsible for all the natural laws and for creation itself, regardless of their understanding of the scriptures.

The journeying of creation on Earth, Masud has already explained in his book 'Masud and The Story of Life'. In this work, Masud pieces together everything which we know, or think we know, about creation and evolution. Along this road there were many miracles and, quite often, that which is beyond miraculous. The wonderful thing is, we can see this happening all around us. Nature, from insects to mammals to plants to those that inhabit the mighty oceans, is changing and producing even more miracles all the time. How wonderful it is for us to be able to witness nature all around us, in all its beautiful forms and colours. Every tree is an example of engineering genius that we could hardly conceive of. Every arthropod, the ants, spiders, bees, wasps and the like are not only beautiful designs in their own right, but have an intelligence which is simply stunning for such small creatures. In many of these creatures which we tend to dismiss simply as 'insects' there exists a level of communal intelligence which humans have never attained. Ants and bees are extremely well organised in their own communities where each individual has a role to play and yet, they often display this communal intelligence which allows the colony to act as though it were an individual. This level of intelligence could surely not occur by accident. There would seem to be a distinct directivity to their evolution in such cases.

When we work closely with nature, we receive many benefits. From bees we obtain honey, from cows we obtain milk and many animals have worked alongside man throughout his own development, including wolves and dogs, camels and horses, goats and many more. These relationships with nature and animals benefit us spiritually as well. We often form close relationships with the animals alongside of us. Such a relationship is a very precious thing and should be valued highly.

Those that abuse nature however are truly dishonoured as to abuse nature is to abuse the creator of nature. Some men are cruel and inconsiderate towards animals under their command. Some are destructive of the natural landscapes around them for no reason. Such abuse is ultimately returned to them as they are abusing life itself. When we do interact with nature, we should surely be grateful that we have the opportunity to do so. Masud often thought this when walking quietly through the mountains near his home. Every rock, every tuft of grass, every small pool, every tree of every kind, the hawks and buzzards which he would see flying so high, the magnificent views which he enjoyed from up on high. These were all things that warmed his heart and made him feel grateful to be alive. He was surely privileged to see, taste and smell these wonderful creations of the natural world. He failed to understand how any man could not be similarly affected by such things. Yes, Masud appreciated and respected the natural world around him and all which it brought to him. As Masud would say, Alhamdulillah.

Understanding

And so, it is important for every man woman and child to understand the importance of nature and the natural world. When walking in the mountains, by a river or in the desert, we must understand that we are simply a part of the nature around us. Like the grains of sand, our lives are blown this way and that. Like the river, we undertake the journeying to our own last day. Like the mountains, we may kiss the clouds and feel the natural elements around us. And, when we interface with animals, we must realise that we are just like them. We are all children of the higher intelligence and of evolution. Yes, we are Allah's children as surely as the crow that comes to the fields. As surely as the camel who shares our load. As surely as the goat or cow who gives us milk. As surely as the dragon fly or the bee. As surely as the grass that grows on the mountain. As all creation in fact. We are kin to the natural world.

And we shall return to the natural world when our time has come, as does everything in creation at one point or another. It follows then that we should develop a respect for and an affinity with all of nature. When we see a colony of ants building their nest, we must think of them as our little brothers and sisters. When we see the bee returning to the hive, we must give him a silent welcome back. When we make use of our horse or camel or ox, we must remember that they see and feel things, just as we do and that they often understand much more than we think they do. Indeed, it is not unusual for a man to have an almost telepathic relationship with his horse or camel as both animals have long memories and appreciate when they are shown kindness. Thus, they become loyal companions.

There is another sort of understanding which we should have at present but which we don't seem to have, except in small isolated cases. And that is the protection of natural environments. Some small initiatives, such as clearing reefs, are useful enough, nut there exists a plethora of commercial organisations posing as charities who claim that they are reversing global warming or protecting the oceans and so on. This is all nonsense of course and all these organisations are really doing is collecting money from those with no scientific background or understanding. On every page of their web sites is the word 'Donate' usually written in large letters and their donation applications often default to collecting monthly payments. This is fraud in its most revolting form as most of these organisations can show no proof of anything which they have actually done themselves. On the back of this are many Government 'kwangos' set up to pay huge salaries to a select group of dishonest individuals. On their web sites, the word 'donate' will also be spread liberally around, again defaulting to monthly payments. They will also claim to be saving the planet or stopping global warming. The amounts of money collected in this fraudulent manner can be absolutely huge and vast amounts have simply disappeared with nothing to show for it. Masud is very aware of these dishonourable fraudsters. They are unworthy as human beings and cause far more trouble than they solve by deliberately peddling incorrect scientific information. Anyone who has studied the geosciences will know this to be true.

However, there is always something we can do to coexist with nature properly at a local level. For those with gardens, for example, they can allow the grass to grow higher and thus attract insects which, in turn, will attract birds. If one has space, the creation of a small pond will attract a myriad of creatures which will seem to come from nowhere. You may consider having a small beehive, in which case, you will be rewarded with fresh honey as a gift in kind. Feed the birds. Observe the behaviour of the different species and allow for them as best you can. If you are out in the wilds of a forest and you come across larger mammals, speak to them gently and observe their response. There will always be a response whether they be wild horses, bears, wolves, elk or any other creature. All of these creatures are capable of interfacing with you in an intelligent manner, if you give them the chance. Most humans simply do not understand this fact, but it is certainly true. And nearly all creatures remember human contact, especially if it is compassionate, sometimes for many years. There is a wealth of good scientific information to support this claim. However, we must beware of the fraudsters, who are everywhere. They all have quite plausible looking web sites but, if you scrutinise them closely, you will find little or no proof of any associated activity. But they all want your money, preferably in monthly payments.

Masud is well aware of the many fraudsters but also aware that there is always something we can do on a personal level in order to respect and work with nature. And nature is full of surprises. One interesting factor which is well documented is the altruism that often exists within the animal world. This exists within species and even between species where one animal will take it upon itself to look after, care for and befriend another. This is particularly interesting as it shows that animals not only have a great ability to reason and to solve problems, but that they also feel compassion. This may be encouraged by anyone who is working with animals or even those who have animals as pets. It has also been noticed that many animals have a sense of the aesthetic. They admire beautiful things. Masud has many times witnessed a dog or a horse simply looking up at the sky and the clouds, or at some beautiful scene. It is clear that they enjoy the fruits of nature just as do those humans who understand the essence of nature. This feeling of belonging to nature and the natural world is a beautiful feeling for those who understand. In some cultures, there is a belief that humans belong to the land. The land does not belong to them. They simply dance upon it for their allotted term and then they are gone, but the land remains. It may be that, one day, we all shall be gone, but the land shall remain and will slowly heal.

So strive to understand nature from every perspective and be kind to all of Allah's children, whatever form they take. The natural world is the only true world.

Civilisation

It is a word which is used in many different contexts, but what exactly is civilisation? If we take it to mean those leading a civilised lifestyle then much of the current world and its human population would not qualify for the term. The word is sometimes used in the context of describing a particular era; a particular people at a particular point in time. For example, we may refer to the ancient Egyptian civilisation. We might thus label them because they had a lifestyle which appreciated the arts and which created beautiful and magnificent monumental buildings. Similarly, we might consider the ancient Greeks as civilised as they brought us a good deal of philosophy and were also artistic in many ways. But would we consider the first wave of Mongols as civilised? Or the Nazis? or the Israelis? or the Americans? or the Turks during the last throws of the Ottoman Empire?. All of these were highly capable and enjoyed extravagant lifestyles, but that surely does not make them civilised. During the renaissance period in Europe there was a wave of artistic and literary output which would certainly qualify as civilised and the great composers of the Viennese period certainly raised the perception of what we mean by civilisation. Haydn,

Mozart and Beethoven, between them created a new world pattern of higher civilisation for others to follow. Beethoven in particular, raised this to a peak which the human race would never realise again.

Today, we have technology and a plethora of expensive toys for the wealthy to enjoy while millions of others are living in strife and poverty. We surely cannot call this a civilised way of living. Indeed, civilisation has been replaced by the all encompassing greed culture which has been pioneered and exported largely by one nation. This one nation has effectively seized control of most of the world, mostly by stealth or by backing other, evil regimes. This most certainly could not be considered as civilised.

However, there remain individuals who do produce works which are uplifting and interesting, as Masud does, and these individuals and their work may be considered as civilised. There are also those who are kind and compassionate towards others. These may be considered as civilised. There are those who walk the straight path and who cannot be bought. These may be considered as civilised. There are those who take in orphans and help them to have a fulfilling life. These may be considered as civilised.

And so, it seems we must adjust our definition of the concept of civilisation as it most certainly does not apply at a national level, or a global level. However, it does apply at the individual level. There is a civilisation of like minded, predominantly good people, distributed around the world who are kind, considerate and respectful of others and who do their best to help those immediately around them. These we may certainly consider as civilised.

Future historians may refer to our times as a civilisation of sorts, but they too will have to adjust their definition of the term. Masud found that, looking around him today, there was little that he would call civilised, although he did respect the civilised nature of the few who stand away from the herd and who proffer kindness and compassion towards others. These are those who are truly civilised.

Laws

We have had defined laws at least since the time of Hammurabi (1792-1750 BC) whose codes of law were based loosely upon the Sumerian system. Hammurabi's codes in Babylon were explicitly written on both clay tablets and on at least one diorite stele which has since been found. There are 282 of them which, together, cover most aspects of life and transactions in ancient Babylon. However, it is likely that the ancient Egyptians also had codes of law which stretched back even further. We know, for example, that they were pedantic about recording transactions and how people were paid for their work, so it is likely that there were laws written somewhere which governed these things. However we lost much of the knowledge of ancient Egypt during the fire that destroyed the library at Alexandria. This great library, thought to have been suggested and supervised by Demetrius of Phalerum was supposed to house a copy of every book in the world. Consequently, a huge number of Egyptian scrolls were sent there for copying. It seems that most of them never returned and so, in what was a tragedy for humanity, we lost a considerable amount of knowledge appertaining to ancient Egypt.

In England, Henry II (1154-1189) set a precedent by establishing a formal parliament in Westminster where Royal Courts were established. These were available to lords and freemen but not available to serfs. The legal processes and content of the common law continued to be refined and, in 1215, the Magna Carta broke new ground and established common rights for the barons, freemen and all, effectively limiting the power of the King. King John died the next year and Henry III came to the throne, but the Magna Carta had had a dramatic effect upon English Common Law. The English Civil War (1624-1649) finally served to make parliament the primary source of power and not the monarchy, with the result that English Common Law would be refined and further developed. In between times, the Tudors had a law based on the King's Law, although this was sometimes met with scepticism, depending upon who you were. It is interesting that in Shakespeare's play Henry VI are the words "First, we kill all the lawyers" which might be said to sum up the attitude of the common man to the law at that time. Nevertheless,

English Common Law and the English legal system became refined and established to the point that many other countries were pleased to adopt it as their own system. Today, it is a complex affair and, as any complete set of legal books will show, it references a great many precedents and covers an enormous scope.

And so, nearly every country has a properly established legal system and a veritable army of lawyers. One might reasonably ask that, if the law is so clear, why do we need this army of lawyers, all charging very high fees. The answer of course is that the law often comes up against cases which are not so clear, or is often challenged by clever lawyers who try to manipulate it on behalf of their clients. Consequently, the legal system and the concept of justice are very often two different things. Furthermore, the law serves different stratas of the community differently. Those with unlimited funds and who are well connected will undoubtedly receive different treatment at the hands of the law.

Charles Dickens parodied the law in several of his books, in one case having the Beadle declare that 'the law is an ass'. Gilbert and Sullivan's first comic opera was Trial by Jury which did the same and, of course, in The Mikado there is a very interesting slant on the law. This is all just relating to English Law. No doubt a similar situation exists in many other countries, whereby ordinary decent citizens do not always consider that they are treated fairly by their particular legal system which, in some cases, is further complicated by the links with religion. If religion effectively becomes the law, this can be dangerous as most religions are founded upon events which occurred more than 2000 years ago. Some would argue that this is a good thing, while some will hold that it may be cruel and barbarous in today's world. In any event, the law is the law and citizens would do well to abide by it.

Society

Linked to all of this is the concept of society. The word may be used to describe a collection of individuals. Such a collection may be large, such as a nation, or may be smaller, such as a group of individuals with a shared interest. There are many professional societies in which learned and qualified individuals may get together on a regular basis in order to discuss their particular interests and to acknowledge any new developments or discoveries. The Geological Society and The Royal Society in London are good examples of this. Most advanced countries have such things.

Unfortunately, there are a great many sham societies who just wish to take money from members and offer them little or nothing in return. Masud considers these as fraudulent and unworthy, but beware, there are more of them than you can shake a stick at. There are trade associations which are similarly variable. They all claim to represent their members and will usually have something like an annual conference, for which their members will usually have an additional cost. These are surely self serving entities which have no respect for their members at all. They just want their annual subscriptions. Many unscrupulous individuals have become very wealthy by establishing such vehicles. The genuine type of professional society however is a good thing where interested individuals may come together under a joint interest.

Then there is the use of society to describe the current status quo within a given state or country. Huge assumptions are made in this context and there is a good deal of psychological manipulation in order to have everyone conform to a politically correct model. Some will follow the herd readily enough, while some will remain independent and capable of reasoning for themselves.

Traditionally, the distinction between societies was often made upon the differences between them, either in culture or development. However, the word is bandied around much more freely now and can mean almost anything in relation to human activities or assemblages. There is the further complication of one society copying another in habit, often influenced by films or other art forms, although they can never quite duplicate their ideals as their underlying culture is often quite different. And so we get, on the one hand, the almost ubiquitous use of technology and consumption of popular artifacts, mixed with regional traits and customs which still serve to separate such societies. For example, the use of mobile phones is so well spread that it is almost global, with very few regions that are not covered in one way or another. This is of course very big business for a handful of suppliers. Similarly, mobile computing devices such as laptop computers and tablets are sourced fro just a handful of suppliers with operating systems mainly from just two suppliers worldwide. This is clear restrictive practice and such monopolies should not be allowed, but the organisations concerned are not known for their morality of fair dealing. And so societies are often manipulated by the supply chain and consumerism. This fact has been exploited by unscrupulous organisations and Government agencies for many years.

In 1969, Kenneth Clark (Lord Clark 1903-1983) made an iconic TV series named simply 'Civilisation'. It is often held as the best series ever made for TV anywhere in the world. It was a personal view of Lord Clark's understanding of how civilisation came into being, what it's high points were and where it looked like it was going. In the series, he noted much fine architecture, art, sculpture and, of course music, which often reflects the societies which create it quite well. His view, like that of Masud, was that Beethoven was the high point. Not just of music, but of civilisation itself. We simply never got any better than that.

Others will hold that we have advanced from a technology perspective, but have we, really? Masud has doubts. We have learned how to manufacture goods at lower cost and sell them for higher cost. We have learned how to force people to accept cashless societies, we have learned how to rob citizens of their privacy, individualism and pride, we have learned how to make more efficient chemical weapons and, indeed, weapons of all kinds including weapons of mass destruction. We have similarly advanced the general face of politics whereby it is now acceptable for politicians to lie openly, to make private deals while in office, to deliberately mislead citizens over major events and to make deals with other countries and organisations which are against the interest of citizens.

Masud considered these so called advances carefully. Were they really good for societies and foe civilisation as a whole? He thought not. And, it was interesting that Kenneth Clark's wonderful series, itself, ended on a note of regretful caution.

Politics

When considering politics, many think back to ancient Greece and indeed, the word itself is derived from the Greek word politiká which would have been thought of by the Greeks as 'affairs of the cities'. However, the concept of agreement upon a course of action by group consent, probably goes back much further to the Mesolithic period. Groups of humans, whether single families or larger groups, would have quickly realised that having an agreed plan and following it was better than random day to day action. Masud imagined how, even before fully articulate speech, humans would have easily been able to communicate their intentions and how this would have led logically to groups and heads of groups.

Masud could also imagine how, within any such group of early humans, it would be quite logical to expect one or more individuals to show natural leadership skills and how, probably, one of these individuals was preferred by the majority and henceforth led the group. A similar situation exists with many animals. This would lead to a sort of monarchy. The issue that some would have with this approach is, among humans anyway, the hereditary element where it would be expected that the monarchy would stay with one family. Inevitably this would occasionally lead to conflicts with one powerful family overthrowing another. We saw this happen within ancient civilisations. At this time, when one family ruled for several generations we have called it a dynasty. However, there is an issue with dynasties also in that they tend to become entrenched and, sometimes, the only way of ending them is with revolution and this, in turn, is not always a good thing.

And so, human civilisations developed the idea of electing individuals to powerful positions of government in what was termed a democracy. The ancient Greeks developed this idea in the year 507 BC when the Athenian leader Cleisthenes introduced reforms which he called 'Demokratia' which, in simple terms means giving power to the people. The ancient Greek system remained split into different levels responsible for law making, a council of representatives and the popular courts. Nevertheless, it ensured that ordinary citizens had some sort of say as to their own destiny.

This system might have prevailed but, in Europe, there was much dissension over who was entitled to rule and how. The monarchy had already been weakened to be mere figureheads and countries were governed by Governments who were starting to split into different factors. In Britain, after the American revolution of 1784, William Pitt the Younger became leader of a new 'Tory' party who represented the established country gentry and merchant classes while Charles Fox represented the interests of religious dissenters and reformists. This 'two party' system was quickly adopted back in America and elsewhere but it was an ill considered approach because it guaranteed a degree of political infighting which was, itself, against the interests of any country. The French Revolution also served to illustrate the lunacy of such an approach. This 'party political' system also led more easily to revolutions which would be a good deal more divisive and decisive such as the emergence of the Communist system in Russia.

But there it is. Humans have never had the communal intelligence shown in the insect world and they have allowed party politics to continue unabated until the whole idea has effectively become meaningless. Political leaders are not elected by public consent. They are proposed by political parties and then a charade of elections is undertaken whereby citizens have the choice between two or three unelected potential leaders to choose between, none of whom represent them or their interest. Anyone who does not understand this game and what it really means does not understand politics.

Early humans would have chosen group leaders by consent. Occasionally, no doubt, there would have been conflicts and maybe even fights between potential leaders, but the outcome would have mostly been what the majority wanted. If they were not happy with the decision, then they could simply choose someone else.

This would have been a fair way of going about things and would have ensured that such leaders developed considerable skills of understanding and leadership which could be passed on. When rival groups would meet, their may have been conflict with perhaps one group being subsumed into another and this, together with an understanding of territory, would have led to the formation of geographic and language distinctions which, in turn, would lead to the first countries or nationalities.

The Greeks introduced a more equitable manner of decision making with their Demokratia which, if maintained and developed further might have proved a workable model. However, we then had powerful Monarchies, dissatisfaction with Monarchies and, eventually, the ugly party politics which really just disguises a sort of organisational autocracy which is most definitely not in the interests of citizens. And yet, many of the world's citizens still believe that they live within a democracy. They do not.

Corruption

As Masud had come to understand, in most of these systems there is a loophole which allows corruption to creep in. Perhaps this is a component of the human psyche but, if so, it is a particularly ugly component. Corrupt Monarchies were reasonably easy to deal with. Either a rival Monarchy would come and unseat them, or the Monarch would be quietly removed from power and replaced by agreement. However, party politics effectively opened the door to rampant corruption and this has, as Masud had discovered, reduced most of the world now to countries effectively being managed by gangsters often referring to themselves as 'the organisation' while a head of state is appointed as a puppet to iterate a succession of meaningless speeches and promises, all written for them by the organisation and none of which are adhered to. The constitution of the organisation varies from country to country. Often it is comprised of a small consortium of super wealthy, powerful families, aided and abetted by a handful of huge multi-national commercial companies, most of which originate from just two or three countries.

The organisation may indeed call itself a Government and, in fact, it is, but it does not behave in the way that citizens believe it does. One of the tactics used by the organisation is what the Americans call 'lobbying'. In the 80s, Masud discovered, for example, that there were several thousands of American lobbyists in the EU. What were they doing there and what were they 'lobbying' for. Perhaps it was no surprise that from then onwards EU countries all gradually adopted American IT systems and gave concessions for American retail chains to be present in nearly every town. Furthermore, giant American companies received all manner of tax concessions with some of them evading tax to the degree that they were effectively paying no tax at all. But then, as Masud also understood, this was all carefully planned within the 'New American Century' document which was published shortly after the second World War and then revised and republished once again. Most of Europe and much of South East Asia has been corrupted in this way while, in other countries, they have developed their own brand of corruption which has sometimes been expressed hand in hand with violence.

This political corruption also deliberately causes conflict and wars as, as the Americans were also quick to realise, war is good business for the organisation, as is narcotics, prostitution, alcoholism and other such vices. This quite horrible landscape is the stuff of modern politics. Governing countries and looking after the interests of citizens has little to do with it.

There are, of course, a few exceptions, where countries are run quite well and where corruption, of any sort, is frowned upon. Masud also understood this well enough. Unfortunately, in the modern world, they are the exception. It would be hoped that other countries would note their example and try to follow it. However the 'organisation' has such a strong grip on things that this is impossible, especially as it hides behind the pretence of democracy and an elected leader. Such elections are recollective of the sort of farces which were once a form of popular entertainment between the war years. Indeed, the wonderful comic opera writers Gilbert and Sullivan would no doubt have managed to parody our current world political systems and their rife corruption quite well. When they were active, in Victorian times, things in Britain were run along much better lines. Thank goodness they cannot see what is happening now.

Masud realised that there was another aspect to all of this. What one might refer to as human evolution. We have had the Renaissance period, the Age of Discovery, the Age of Enlightenment and we seem to have now entered into another darker age of what Masud often calls the 'greed culture'. It has, unfortunately, spread like an ugly virus across the world causing suffering, tragedy and want in an age when such things could easily be avoided. Such a sad indictment for the human race and one which may well lead towards the last day.

Technology

Masud mused that the word 'technology' would adopt a quite different complexion depending upon geography, time and utility. The ancient Egyptians certainly had a great deal of technology. They had perfected the craft of ship building, they were great mathematicians who also had an uncommon grasp of geometry, they understood the movements of the planets and the associated cycles, they manufactured a wide range of goods for practical everyday use and employed a wide range of tools. They were equally proficient in the arts with master sculptors and a plethora of musicians and singers, many of them female and, of course scribes whose written work was superbly executed. This was a case of technology serving the requirements of society. One could make similar comments about the Sumerians, Babylonians, the Harappan culture and several others.

It was the setting of these trends which carried over into later civilisations, the Romans representing a sort of intermediary step between the old and new worlds. The new world adopted what was useful from the old, at least as best as they could but, unfortunately the level of skill and craftsmanship did not always make the transition. The world has never seen the equal of the

Egyptian sculptors who created such beautiful objects or their stone masons who could work with such precision. Sumerian and Babylonian mathematicians would undertake calculations in their head or with variations of the cuneiform writing system which most mathematicians could not attempt today. Masud felt it important to understand that these ancient peoples were using technology to complement their own skills. They were not reliant upon it. This is a key difference between them and us.

Throughout history, there have been some inventions which have had a significant impact. The wheel is obviously one of them and it is impossible to state with any accuracy who really invented it. It is often attributed to Mesopotamia and either the Akkadians or Sumerians, but then the ancient Egyptians were using it as far back as archaeological records show. And, of course, there were potters wheels and spinning wheels.

Gunpowder was another invention which would have a dramatic change upon warfare and conflict although this change took longer to become effective than some assume. It triggered a great rush of technological activity in the design of weapons which, unfortunately, reflects a nastier side of the human psyche. We always seem to have the funds to develop technology with which to kill each other. Masud thought much about this. The creation of the first atomic bomb, to which scientists such as Jacob Bronowski and Albert Einstein both contributed on the understanding that it would never actually be used but simply held as a deterrent, was a truly evil example of this. But surely, men of the calibre of Bronowski and Einstein understood that politicians could never be trusted? Especially American politicians? One would hope so. Ever since that horrible time, weapons of mass destruction have been designed, one after another, each more terrible than its predecessor.

The printing press was another invention that had an enormous impact upon the world. The use of the first proper printing press is often attributed to Johannes Gutenberg in Europe in 1452. However the ancient Chinese were printing with wooden block characters from around 1086 and, not long after this in Korea, they were using movable type. As with many important inventions, we shall probably never know who really first had the idea but, certainly, Gutenberg's press was practical and repeatable. Once the principle had been established, advances would come very quickly. The advent of metal type and mechanical typesetting brought precision and repeatability to page creation and the roller mechanisms of printing presses became more sophisticated. Typesetting was letter by letter and, of course had to be accurate. To prepare and print the pages of an entire book was a major operation and typesetters, the men who put each sentence together letter by letter, were highly skilled and highly paid. Each metal letter was stored in a special grid like open cabinet with larger spaces for the most commonly used letters and these metal letters were reused again and again until the serifs or edges became visibly worn. And then in 1896 came the Linotype machine. This was a different concept whereby an entire line of type was produced by the operator 'typing' into a machine. Each line was a solid slug of metal which would be used just once and then melted down for manufacture of other lines. This was perfect for the newspaper industry which was thriving at the time.

In 1904 the thermionic valve was invented and this quickly became the basis of the electronics industry. It enabled the practical development of the wireless radio receiver which became very popular. Valves themselves became more efficient and more powerful. Demand for them also grew, about tenfold from 1910 to 1920. The valve also enabled high quality amplifiers to be built and, together with efficient, horn loaded loudspeakers and high quality turntables, gave birth to the High Fidelity industry.

The field effect transistor was first proposed in 1925 by Austrian Hungarian physicist Julius Edgar Lilienfeld and patents were filed in Canada. But this work was largely ignored until the 1940s when researchers at the Bell Laboratories built some working transistors according to Lilienfeld's ideas. Then, in 1947, the transistor was claimed as an invention by William Shockley, Walter Brattain and John Bardeen who were credited with the idea which quite clearly, with hindsight, was not theirs. But Bell Laboratories was the research arm of the powerful AT&T company and so the claim stood. In any event, the transistor effectively replaced the valve as it was easier and much less expensive to manufacture. Then the Japanese adopted the transistor with enthusiasm and started to build a plethora of transistor radios, amplifiers and other equipment. Masud found it interesting to note that many audio enthusiasts, even today, much prefer the sound quality of valves. The human ear can detect minute characteristics of sound and the inherent smoothness and warmth of the valve sound is much more realistic than that from transistor only equipment.

With transistors came physically smaller circuits which enabled smaller, lighter electronic devices of all kinds including, eventually the first electronic portable calculator. These devices started to be designed in the 1960s but it was the Sinclair Executive, in 1972 which really introduced the idea to the public. This elegant, hand held device was truly pocketable and worked well with an LED display of the calculation. Other Sinclair models quickly followed including the Cambridge and Oxford varieties. They were all very interesting devices.

It was logical to extend the capabilities of the electronic calculators to larger, more powerful machines which would be the first really practical computers. The IBM personal computer launched in 1981 had a huge marketing campaign behind it and many thought that this was the first practical computer. It was not. Masud realised that many outside of Britain were unaware that an English lady named Sophie Wilson was way ahead of the IBM company with its huge budgets and myriad of engineers. Sophie, more or less on her own, designed the Acorn computer in 1978 in Cambridge, England. In 1979 the Acorn Model 1 was released, then in 1980 the Acorn Atom and the BBC Micro was designed by Acorn in 1981. This was an advanced computer inspired by the BBC's drive to make school children computer literate. The BBC Micro had a wealth of connectivity options and many thousands of students learned computing on a BBC Micro machine. Sophie then went on to design the ARM processor in 1985. She remained ahead of all the big budget companies. In 1986 Acorn designed and built the BBC Master Compact computer which, even today, looks like a modern computer.

The original conception of the personal computer was, of course, to undertake complex calculations for specific purposes. In order to do this, an operating system was used to present a series of command options to the user who could, with these commands, write a computer script, or programme, in order to undertake some repetitive task or other. BASIC and CP/M were such systems which introduced many to computing. There was much anguish and law suits when Microsoft introduced MS DOS which was almost identical to CP/M with just one or two different commands. This is what they licensed to IBM for the IBM PC and which, of course made the young company extremely wealthy extremely quickly. But it should have been credited to the man who actually designed it. Both BASIC and CP/M were designed by Gary Kildall in the interests of making computing easy enough for anyone. Many would hold that this practice of stealing other people's ideas and marketing them as your own, was the foundation and ongoing strategy of Microsoft as a company. Kildall went on to found Digital Research with his wife and there was a later version of DR-DOS which was far superior to the Microsoft version but, of course, Digital Research did not have the IBM contract.

In any event the focus of personal computing, as driven by Microsoft and Apple Mackintosh, quickly moved away from the scientific to the hobbyist and then the mainstream market including the provision of computer games. Many see this as a wasted opportunity. What saved the day were two quite useful applications, the word processor and the spreadsheet and these formed the backbone of many computer operations in small and medium sized companies, but there were always the private enthusiasts who also used these tools. There were also mainframe computers which sometimes filled entire rooms and which were used by Governments and industry to perform large calculations very quickly.

But the world has since seen a major shift in the use of computer technology. Now it is used to design manufactured goods to be much cheaper to make while selling for much higher prices. It is used to inflict levels of surveillance upon ordinary decent people which would not have been believed by George Orwell or

Aldus Huxley. It is used for the creation of evil computer 'games' which are characterised simply by violence and hatred of anything that was considered good or uplifting. It is used to falsify Government elections and to deliberately mislead citizens. It is used to replace terrestrial broadcasting, giving monopolies to giant corporations who ultimately use their channels for propaganda purposes.

Furthermore the modern domestic computers (mostly laptops) are poorly made devices, far inferior in performance to those of a decade or so back, which do not offer a choice of operating systems and have virtually no storage and very little memory.

This almost complete destruction and control of the computer industry, dominated by two American giant corporations, is reflected in other industries where amalgamations and takeovers have served to lower the quality of all products, restrict choice to the consumer and yet make the super wealthy companies in control even more super wealthy, their directors living billionaire lifestyles as a result of cheating consumers.

Aspirations

The 'New American Century' document was referred to earlier and this plan has been enacted and largely completed, with just one or two territories not yet fully under control. However, even that odious document did not spell out the evil which has been enacted throughout most of the world since that time in pursuance of the aspirations expressed within it. The all pervasive push towards 'junk food' which has served to give whole generations health problems, including obesity which, in turn, lead to psychological problems. The deliberate dumbing down of education (for the masses) in order to render them simply as consumer robots who have no interest in anything. The rewriting of history in order to eliminate anything which was noble and good. The pretence that anything of value was invented in America (actually, the opposite is mostly true). The unrelenting bribery and corruption in and among Governments to ensure that evil pertains in almost every territory. The cheating of consumers, forcing them to pay much more than is necessary for even basic goods and foodstuffs. The encouragement of the global greed culture where everyone fit enough to do so is just out to rob everyone else. And this is all undertaken under the pretence that we are a civilised global society.

This is what technology has largely been used for in the last half century. The notion that technology is always good or used for good is a heavily flawed one, as has been shown. Some will argue, ah, but what about advances in medical technology? Well, there have been some, but very few which may be called genuinely useful advances, especially given the sums that have been diverted world wide towards medical research, and the amount which has been taken from the public under such pretence. We have, of course, had no expense spared in the creation and deployment of man made viruses and these undoubtedly originated from the country who, in the 1960s, was boasting that they had more chemical warfare agents than the rest of the world put together. As Masud knows, this country was not China. Then there are the equally evil vaccines which, it is no secret, have killed more people than the virus ever did, even given that variations of the virus continue to be re-released on a regular basis.

This covert chemical warfare is all part of another aspiration to exert control over the global population. Those who finally isolated the vaccines were ostracised from the professional world, losing their jobs and prevented from working anywhere, even though they were accomplished and respected scientists. Why was this? It has since been shown that in addition to the Graphene oxide which was responsible for blood clots, strokes and heart attacks, the vaccines contained a concoction of metallic trace elements which had nothing to do with medicine or healing. But these trace elements accumulate in the body and do not go away. So what are they doing there? It has been suggested that they vibrate at certain frequencies (as all things do) and that these frequencies have been shown to coincide with those of 5G mobile networks. This is very interesting because there has been an almost fanatical push towards the establishment of 5G Mobile networks almost everywhere and many technologists have argued that this is wrong because we simply do not need them.

Existing 4G networks are already more capable than is really necessary for mobile communication, so why do we need anything else? There is clearly another agenda being pursued here and it is undoubtedly one which is not in the common interest.

The indigenous people of South Africa, the Aborigines in Australia and some of the First Nations people in Canada and North America have all complained and have claimed that they are being used as human 'guinea pigs' in order to experiment with these viruses and related vaccines. It is hard to argue against these claims and it makes Masud wonder about the real aspirations behind all of this.

Science

For the outgoing generation and their immediate predecessors, science was a very interesting thing. There were proper scientists who were undertaking interesting work for the common interest and the common good. However, things are very different now and may be said to be split into two groups. In the first group, which we may call popular science, everything is focused upon what we already know and everything is dumbed down to the mass audience. Furthermore, everything in this group, including a multitude of TV programmes, is presented by inexperienced individuals with a mock enthusiasm as if they had discovered something interesting. This is not science. It barely qualifies as pseudo science. This is particularly objectionable when dealing with history, archaeology and nature. Presenters, often American, try to inject 'drama' into that which has none, in order to fool viewers that they are uncovering something special. It is the same in many popular science books which simply regurgitate the same old stuff with enhanced images and text which is uninteresting and dumbed down to a very low level. In literature, there are at least a few exceptions, but the interested reader will have to go looking for them.

The other branch of science is what is not presented to the public as it is mostly the pursuit of evil, either to exert absolute control over citizens under the guise of 'security' or for the design of chemical and physical warfare. There is also a very active 'cyber science' thread which is mostly looking to interfere with either individual, group or even national activity. Indeed, the amount of surveillance that has been introduced in the west is very disturbing indeed.

Given this situation, one wonders what the many hundreds of thousands, if not millions, of qualified scientists are actually doing. Some will be employed in the evil branch of science, some will obtain positions within the media and many will remain in academia, whiling away their time doing practically nothing. This may sound like a damning conclusion to scientists but, as Masud has learned, it is largely true. Most of the scientific inventions of value, which enhanced human knowledge, were undertaken more than a century ago, some of them several centuries back. Since then, there have been a few inventions of minor interest and a few refinements to existing knowledge, but really not that much. Except, of course, in the evil sciences. It would be nice to see some genuine breakthroughs in either the natural or physical sciences. Alas, elder scientists who are knowledgeable in their subjects will wonder where these breakthroughs are.

Projections

Masud found it interesting that many of the ancient civilisations had some sort of vision for where humanity was headed. The ancient Egyptians often referred to the 'end of days' which, they predicted, would be preceded by a period of chaos wherein evil would often be portrayed as 'normal' or 'good' and good would be portrayed as 'evil'. Looking at the current global culture of greed, it is hard to disagree with their prediction. The Christian Bible speaks of a 'judgment day' and all Muslims will be aware of 'the last day' as referenced within the Holy Quran. Other cultures, at various times seemed to have similar beliefs. Individual men and women, from Mesolithic times onward have no doubt wondered about such things.

Those who have studied evolution will understand that the fossil record indicates that 95% or more of all known species are actually extinct. And yet, the fossil record that has been available to us no doubt reflects a mere fraction of all the species that have walked on this Earth and then, subsequently, have disappeared. The majority of species, it seems, are destined for extinction. This raises interesting questions with regard to the human species. In evolutionary terms we are very much a late comer. A recently introduced species which has swarmed out of control and which has dramatically changed the face of the world. Some describe the human species as a virus upon the face of the Earth. The inexorable rise of human activity and associated impact, coupled to the exponential rise in population is indeed worrying from several points of view.

A little over a decade ago, Masud met with a lady who, at the time, was often referred to as the world's leading biologist. She had spent a lifetime studying the emergence and continuance of life. Masud asked her how long she thought the human species could continue before disaster might overtake it. She answered the question with a question. "How long do you think, Masud?" The latter replied that he was struggling to see current human policies lasting for more than a century before something broke and would cause huge upheaval. The lady laughed. "No Masud" she replied, "fifty years". Masud thought this a slightly pessimistic view at the time, but it is now starting to look more feasible. At any rate, human activity and current policies cannot continue indefinitely. We are already seeing the ancient Egyptian prediction of chaos becoming a reality. It is surely time that world leaders got together and discussed such matters in an intelligent manner. Some of them do get together and have conferences on 'environmental issues' but this is largely for public consumption. At the same time, the nations which they represent are destroying natural habitats at an alarming rate and this activity will have knock on effects which the politicians will eagerly embrace and call 'climate change'. Then they will have more conferences, raise more taxes and so on. The merry go round continues with the international carousel of pretence spinning nicely.

Of course, there are those who are sincerely trying to protect nature and preserve what they can of the natural world. They appreciate, as does Masud, that we are all a part of nature. We shall never destroy nature completely as it is based upon the natural laws which come from the higher intelligence, but we may well destroy ourselves. Masud thought of all the horrible wars and conflicts currently raging and killing millions of innocent individuals. Most of these are deliberately being kept alive as war is 'good business'. The lies that are fed to the media while atrocities and crimes against humanity are being committed by those who can do so, are themselves part of the evil. And it is this evil which will be the destructive agent for the human species.

Those who can see this will try their best to be as self sufficient as possible and it may well be that we shall see a number of smaller communities cropping up which will become more supportive and also something of an inspiration for younger generations. This would be fine even though, in some ways, it would seem like returning to an almost medieval way of life. The issue with this of course is that it will only be possible in certain areas of certain countries. Those which still have a natural agricultural facility will be able to do this. Even those that might not have such a facility but which do have arrable land could return to this sort of lifestyle. However, the bulk of the world's populations live in cities where this would simply not be viable. There is also the question of access to fresh water and this is likely to become a very serious matter in future years. In many developed countries they have been relying upon recycled water now for decades and still the water table is lowering and reservoirs are inadequate for the task. This is very serious indeed and could well become a triggering point for violent developments.

Many, no doubt, discuss such matters privately but what are Governments doing to protect the future of humanity? They undoubtedly have plans for the future, some of which they would not wish to be common knowledge.

The Journeying

And so, it seems that human beings were always wondering about the future, both the immediate future and the longer term future for the human species. On a personal level, many see life as a journey. It has been so for as long as anyone can remember. A journey in which we, as individuals, are tested as to our honesty, charity, compassion and general decency as human beings. In most cultures there has been a belief in the afterlife and that our journeying in this life is simply a preparation for what follows. If we prove equal to the tests and challenges of this life, then we shall enjoy a glorious afterlife. If we prove unequal to them, we shall not. The ancient Egyptians depicted this idea beautifully with the weighing of the heart ceremony whereby, upon leaving this world, the individual was taken by the hand by Anubis to the great scales where, on one side was placed their heart, on the other, a feather representing all of the good deeds that they performed in their mortal lives. If the scales balanced, they were admitted into the court of Osiris and Isis and everlasting life. If not, their heart was tossed to a waiting demon who consumed it and they simply ceased to exist. A lovely idea. The scriptures from biblical times take a different slant but the idea of our mortal lives being a test, reverberates throughout, and in isolated cultures where there is a belief in The Great Spirit.

However, our individual journeying is simply a part of the larger species journeying and it is the latter that we should especially be thinking about now. If we reflect upon the ancient civilisations, it is clear that there is very little of value which they did not have. The ancient Egyptians, Sumerians and Babylonians had an advanced understanding of mathematics, they understood the movements of the stars and could navigate by them (as could the Bedu who were probably the precursors to the ancient Egyptians), they had fine linen and robes, they enjoyed fruits and staples as well as game, they knew how to find water (or set up cairns) they built fine buildings and they traded with each other readily enough. There was of course occasional conflict, but none of them were trying to take over the world and any fighting was mostly hand to hand. They were also literate and enjoyed singing and dancing, always ready to celebrate something or other. Similarly the First Nation tribes in Canada and the North Americas, while not quite as advanced in some ways, had nevertheless developed a way of life which, for them, was sustainable. Similarly so in Europe and South East Asia.

Things might have ambled along quite nicely if it were not for the Age of Discovery and, especially, the Industrial Revolution. Both accelerated trade and development, including human population and the destruction of natural habitats. Developments since then have mostly been concerned with business and the creation of large, or sometimes huge corporations and organisations which are self-serving. Citizens are thus reduced to mere consumers to support these large organisations including, of course, the overweight Government and related agencies in every country.

Our journeying as a species has been dramatic and fast. We have swarmed over the globe, preyed upon its natural resources and destroyed a great deal of natural habitat, replacing it with great cities of large towers and roads. But has this improved the quality of life for humans? It is a good question. It has provided more distractions with the availability of a myriad of toys and instant 'entertainment' via what used to be televisions and which are now merely large screen computer devices, the 'smart' variants of which are used to gather user data, viewing habits and so on which is then sold on to whoever wants it. This ensures that, even if the suppliers boast hundreds of channels, the content is the same on most of them. Many of these devices can also act as cameras, effectively looking into the living rooms of consumers and gathering more information about them. This is a form of covert surveillance which should surely be illegal, but which is not. Is this progress?

The term 'progress' has become synonymous with progress and extra profits for the giant companies who are accelerating the destruction, not only of our planet, but of our independence and dignity as human beings. This shall of course continue unchallenged as much of it comes from the same source as most of the violence and conflict which has existed over the past century.

But what of our journeying as a species? Are we approaching what the ancient Egyptians called the 'end of days'? We certainly have the chaos and hypocrisy which they predicted would be a precursor to this. From a purely evolutionary perspective, the current global situation is indeed cause for concern and Governments might usefully be focussing upon this reality.

Humanity

In this book, Masud has been considering humanity from various perspectives. This is useful and the reader might take each of these chapters and continue their own research upon the topic which Masud has offered to them via his own clear words. By doing so, they shall automatically be building an understanding of the broader landscape of what we have been calling humanity. But what do we really mean by the word 'humanity'? Is it possible to create a simple definition that may be understood and accepted by all?

We may simply describe humanity as being the aggregate of human existence upon the Earth since the time of Homo Erectus and Homo Sapiens. That would be a reasonable description which maintains a distinction between humanity and civilisation. It is an important distinction as the term 'civilisation' may be used in a variety of contexts depending upon who is using it and for what reason.

But there is something more. In the hearts and minds of many individuals, irrespective of their particular level of education, the term 'humanity' takes on an aesthetic which, for them, defines what humanity *should* be. They often equate the term with altruistic qualities which should include compassion for those who suffer, tolerance for those from different backgrounds and kindness to all, regardless of their position. Even this is a simplistic description. For the concept of humanity in the hearts of those who believe in it is ingrained at a very low level as an integral component of the human psyche. In a similar way, the altruistic traits that have often been observed in animals comes, no doubt, from something at this similarly low level.

We may not all be able to describe humanity in clear cut terms but those who understand and believe in it will certainly know in their hearts what it is. They will also have a keenly felt sense of the inhumanity which they see occurring around them. The term 'crimes against humanity' was originally coined to describe the outrageous violence and terror tactics practised under the name of warfare. There was a time, not so long ago, when the world would have agreed that crimes against humanity should never be tolerated. However, today crimes against humanity are being committed year on year and no one is standing up against them. This truth brings into question whether the world's leaders and politicians have simply abandoned any concept of humanity in the interests of greed. It is the same with big businesses and the giant corporations who often like to give the impression that they are supporting humanitarian initiatives, but they are of the hypocrites. In truth, their only interest is greed, profit and more profit, always at the expense of ordinary decent citizens and those who are involved in weapons manufacture, addictive drugs and strong alcohol certainly have much to answer for. The true humanitarians are usually the unobtrusive individuals, from all walks of life, who are simply doing their best to help those immediately around them. If everyone were to adopt this policy, the world would surely be a much nicer place.

And so, it seems that there are but a few who really understand and feel the concept of humanity. They may be found within most cultures, they may be male or female and of any age. They are of those who walk the straight path and who never hesitate to help someone close to them who is in need.

What it Means to be Human

Young people the world over are brainwashed, to one degree or another, to believe that success in life simply means being successful in business or, perhaps, in the popular arts. In one country in particular, youngsters are brainwashed to believe that the *only* thing important in life is to make money. The more the better. Consequently, in this country, those who cheat and steal and make vast fortunes are looked up to and respected, while the poor are despised. Similarly, in the same country, those who achieve success in the popular arts or sports are worshipped as heroes, while those who do not are simply forgotten. This is a truly horrible system which, unfortunately, has been exported throughout most of the world during the past seventy five years or so. Individuals are taught simply to disrespect everyone except those few who are super wealthy, to whom they will bow, curtsy and grovel in the hope of securing some favour. In such a manner those at the top effectively exert absolute control over those beneath them in this artificial social structure. It is a system in which only the evil are ever really happy. The rest live in a state of permanent paranoia. It may come as no surprise that the country from which this system originates has one of the very worst records of violent crime, suicide, substance abuse, alcoholism, obesity and other social ills. The irony is that they seem to believe that they are the best country in the world.

Masud considered that what is important is not how to die wealthy, but how to live like a human being. To do this, one must have the strength of character to reject corruption and to show kindness and compassion to those who are in need, though they be of different cultures or speak in a different tongue. This is particularly so for orphans and widows who may be suffering because of the evil of others. Masud's heart feels particularly for orphans whose lives are turned upside down and often ruined because of the aggression of others. It is not their fault, but they have to pay the price while the aggressors continue to steal cheat and kill their way through life. The first humans, while possibly protective of their families and special places of importance to them, were surely not as insanely greedy and aggressive as their modern counterparts. No, this is the product of countless generations of humans who have learned how to be evil and this characteristic is passed down genetically to subsequent generations. If the first humans were as evil as many are today, it is doubtful that they would have survived that long as a species.

Masud then wondered, how can youngsters be taught how to live like human beings? The education system, in many countries fails badly in this respect. At best, it teaches young students how to pass exams. At worst, and more commonly it teaches them the greed culture and, in certain countries, drills it into them with such a vengeance that they are mere robots by the time they graduate. In many countries, the education system proudly boasts that it takes no hand in moral teaching of any kind as this is outside of their remit. It leaves it to the parents but, if the parents themselves are immoral how shall they teach their children?

Muslims have, of course, the Holy Quran whose guidance, if followed carefully, will certainly help. Christians have the Christian Bible which also teaches the right path. However, as the prophet Muhammad (PBUH) teaches us, there are plenty of hypocrites. Those who do walk the straight path, will take pains to teach their children properly and make sure that, whatever professional accomplishments they accrue, they will remain on the straight path. They will remain as human beings. And they alone will understand what it means to be a human being and what it means to live a worthwhile and honourable life. And they alone shall find true happiness in this life, for happiness comes from making others happy or from comforting them in their hour of need.

There are many examples of this throughout history. One which springs to mind is that, during The Great War, there were a large number of middle class English girls who volunteered to go over to the Western Front and become nurses in the field hospitals there. They were ill equipped, largely untrained and completely unprepared for the horrors that awaited them. And yet, they stood their ground and stayed to help the wounded and dying as best they could. To come from comfortable surroundings to the completely inadequate and insanitary conditions of makeshift field hospitals at the front was something more than a culture shock. But these brave young ladies did not flinch from what they saw as their duty.

During the second war, in bombed out London, people were climbing from the rubble and going to work at their normal jobs. At the end of almost every street would be volunteer ladies with a tea urn, giving out cups of tea and generally cheering people up. Yes, these were of those who knew what it was to live like a human being. There are those behaving similarly today in places such as Palestine, where volunteers are rushing the injured to and from overworked hospitals and doing their best to help extract people from the rubble of bombed buildings. Often these are individuals doing so after their day's work or simply taking time out to help in whatever way they can. Masud and many others understand that the same evil that was behind the second World War is behind the evil and genocide being enacted in Palestine, and it is an evil founded upon greed and control.

Nevertheless, there are those who understand what it means to be a human being. They are dotted around on every continent. The evildoers deride and despise them but this does not deter them in the least. For true humanity comes from within. It comes straight from the heart and cannot be bought or corrupted. Those who understand and practice this will lead worthwhile and fulfilled lives, whatever their particular station in life. And, at the end of their journeying, they shall be content. The evildoers shall never be content for, however much gold they surround themselves with, it will never be enough. They will never know true contentment and love. Those who understand the meaning of humanity will know both and it shall walk with them, on the straight path, for all of their days.

Epilogue

This book has been about humanity. Within its pages, Masud has explored several factors of life which have served to direct the development of human evolution and what some would call civilisation. Taking this approach allows and hopefully inspires the reader to look into these and other areas more deeply. Indeed, as occurred to Masud, several books could be written on the subject and would still leave room for more research. The term 'humanity' as has been discussed, is far from being adequately defined in many minds. Furthermore, in modern times, it is clearly thought of quite differently from how it once was.

Whether early man thought much about the topic is hard to state with any certainty, although very early cave paintings and unfathomable designs show that there was certainly thinking beyond the obvious. By Neolithic times, several cultures were highly advanced, highly organised and lived according to codes which, in the most part, were highly moral, certainly more so than today. The ancient Egyptian 'wisdom texts' provide us with a glimpse of this morality and the desirability of walking the straight path. These were written several thousand years before the Biblical texts which we use today. They encouraged citizens to lead good lives and explained how to do this, often by examples and parables. These texts were usually dictated by the pharaoh, distributed to the main towns and cities and then read allowed to eagerly awaiting citizens. This was a nice idea which worked well in practice and was surely a component of the amazing achievements made at this time.

Later, in Medieval times, sometimes referred to as the 'dark ages' there were Knights who devoted their entire lives to helping others, especially those in distress, and sometimes at the risk of personal danger. And so the idea of humanity was alive and well, even in times which were, themselves, somewhat unpredictable and which were certainly no stranger to evil.

Some would hold that, throughout human history, there has been a struggle between good and evil. Some would further suggest that, currently, evil is winning the battle and that, when it does, we shall see the 'end of days' as variously predicted since Neolithic times. There will be various opinions upon the matter however, one things which is not in doubt, is that as long as one individual understands humanity and what it means to live like a human being, then the concept of reality will remain alive and there will always be hope. As a result of our global community, change in one area often affects all areas, sooner or later. This can be a very bad thing, especially from an economic perspective, as a serious downturn or crash in one area can quickly affect the entire world. It is also a bad thing when the adoption of certain practices which are either immoral, harmful or both and especially by the younger generation, also reverberate around the world at an alarming pace. The evildoers who control the supply chains are of course acutely aware of this and use it to their own advantage, but often against the interest of citizens. The wide adoption of mobile devices which is robbing children of their childhood and brainwashing young and old alike is a good example of this, as is the drive towards cashless societies, the trade in narcotics and more.

The media is also becoming globalised although, it is heavily influenced and controlled by one nation. This is a dangerous development for propaganda purposes and, unfortunately, this is precisely how it is being used. Most of the so called 'social media' is also subject to a huge amount of control in this way. When anyone tries to go against the grain and expose the truth, they are often ostracised for doing so and, in some cases, simply 'eliminated'. All of this (and many more examples could be given) suggests that this globalisation is mostly a very bad thing, at least from the point of view of humanity.

This, in turn, leads us back to our definition of the term and whether we think of humanity as something which serves the best interest of human beings. It would certainly be a hard case to argue with respect to the modern world. Human rights have always been an issue and this seems to be in no way ameliorated by our modern, globalised society. Indeed, while a pretence is maintained in political circles, there remain many flagrant abuses in just about every country. Legal instruments such as the Geneva Convention, which had 195 signatories, are routinely ignored by most of the world when it suits them. There are four primary Geneva Conventions, plus additions, all of which seem to mean absolutely nothing when certain countries wish to either bully their own citizens or attack those of other countries. There are several examples of this inhumanity occurring as this is being written.

And so, we have a term (humanity) and a concept to go with it and although the concept may have changed over the years and is certainly abused from a political perspective, there remain those who have a strong sense of humanity and who, hopefully, will pass this on to their children, along with a love and respect for the natural world in general. We also have those who know how to live like a human being and will do so regardless of what is happening around them. Unfortunately, in the modern world, they represent a minority. A minority which seems further distanced each year and which is, proportionally, very small.

Species Evolution

Given what has been discussed above, what may this mean for the continuation of our species? Those who have studied evolution will appreciate that the vast majority of species of which we have knowledge are now extinct. As we only have the fossil record to guide us and as this disappears after a while, our knowledge in this area is not absolute. However, the evidence within the available fossil record is irrefutable and leads us to the conclusion that most species become extinct. Those that swarm are especially likely to do so.

From an evolutionary perspective, we are a very recent addition to the animal kingdom. Furthermore, we have multiplied at an exponential rate. We have also had a greater impact upon the natural world than any other species of which we are aware. This growth rate and impact are simply not sustainable. Many geoscientists and natural scientists have been saying this for the past century. However, it seems that no one is listening and no Government is proposing any particular plan for the future in this respect. That is not to say that they may not have one. We are now fully aware of the 'American New Century' plan and how this has been, and continues to be enacted. There may be other plans based upon segregation or violence of some kind of which we are not aware.

The artificial focus upon discussions around 'global warming' are simply a smokescreen. Every scientist knows that global warming is a natural phenomenon. This is not the main environmental issue. The primary issue is habitat destruction and the knock on effects that always go with it. Governments and the media pay lip service to the issue while continuing to destroy natural habitats at an alarming rate. Those lucky enough to live in large, more sparsely populated countries may believe that they are immune from any associated issues and their consequences. However, nature also works on a global basis and, what happens in one country, may well have consequences for another.

Mankind has tried to control nature. We have been attempting to control the weather patterns since the 1960s when John Kennedy announced a NASA initiative in America to do just that. We have re-routed rivers and built artificial dams. We have built coastal defences to try to control the oceans. We have cultivated genetic crops and have made artificial copies of almost every natural form of flora. But the main damage that we inflict upon the Earth remains habitat destruction. This is not just destruction of the rain forests or artificially dividing land, but simple things like building over green areas in densely populated small countries such as Britain, or the trend in citizens paving over their gardens and stopping the rain from seeping fully into the groundwater. We are destroying natural habitats on every scale in every country.

One of the very worst impacts we are having is in the oceans. We have been over-fishing for some decades now and, while nature may recover to a degree, there is a limit to this. Furthermore, the techniques we are using, such as long line fishing, are extremely cruel and cause distress and death to many creatures beyond the targeted group. Deep ocean trawling, largely for minerals, also causes terrible destruction to the sediments. These natural sedimentary deposits have been accruing for millions of years and are home to a great many creatures. We are destroying them in a matter of months. Do we think that this will have no knock on effects? It will surely do so. The amount of fuel spilt into the oceans has been colossal, not just from accidents involving oil tankers, but from poorly maintained older diesel vessels of which there are a great many in operation. Then there is the matter of all the rubbish being dumped in the oceans. Actually, this has been occurring for many years and has been highlighted in recent years as much of it now involves plastics. And, of course, all the sewage which is also pumped out into the oceans.

What was once perhaps the most beautiful part of our planet, as well as occupying around 70% of its surface, is now being systematically poisoned and littered with human waste, while its natural inhabitants are being caught and slaughtered at an alarming rate and using horrible methods. This, in a manner, also reflects the inhumanity of humankind. As Masud is aware, a very large book could be written upon the damage we are wreaking within the world's oceans. But the oceans are themselves a conveyor belt of currents which carry nutrients around the globe. They also have a direct effect upon weather patterns due to the water and atmospheric cycles that exist in nature. Any damage that we do to the oceans damages our world. The world in which we all live. But who, politically, is standing up and fighting the cause for this? Nobody. A decade or so back it was proven beyond doubt that high power side sonar devices used by the American Navy were killing marine mammals at an alarming rate. In England, a whole batch of whales and dolphins were washed ashore when American Navy vessels were undertaking experiments with side sonar devices in the English Channel. Post mortem examinations showed that these creatures died agonising deaths with brain haemorrhages and disruptions to other internal organs. This is hardly surprising as the Americans were boasting at the time that they could kill a man at 100 yards with a pulse from a side sonar device. One wonders what sort of evil individual would design such a weapon and what sort of evil individual would deploy it in other people's waters which are known to have a significant presence of marine mammals.

And so, on both land and sea we are destroying habitats hand over fist. Simultaneously, we are multiplying in numbers at a serious rate. We have also taken down most barriers to economic migration in Europe and Britain, already the most congested areas which, in itself is not sustainable. Meanwhile, we continue to commit genocide in Palestine and maintain ongoing conflicts in Yemen, Ukraine and elsewhere. Does this sound like humanity in action? One could hardly think so. The genocide being committed in Palestine by the Israelis and Americans is against all tenets of humanity. Attacks on refugee camps populated by half starved women and children cannot be justified by any use of the term humanity. The repeated unintelligent claim by the Israelis that they thought there were Hamas control points among them beggars belief, and yet the world does nothing.

If this wanton violence, destruction and theft continues then the whole world will descend into the chaos which was predicted by the ancient Egyptians. Literacy will recede, already the mass global culture has largely stopped reading books as they mindlessly watch television which itself has been dumbed down to an alarming level. As they often watch such things on their mobile devices, attention spans are becoming much shorter as they flip between carefully controlled channels which offer no education but plenty of violence. The films being released now seem to be just full of vulgarity and horrible violence. In other words, human civilisation is already descending with the masses remaining ignorant while a few make vast fortunes as they exploit this fact. Even higher education, at University level has, in most countries, been dumbed down and the fact that someone holds a degree these days means very little, especially as a large proportion of such degrees are in the arts.

These are all indicators that civilisation is going backwards. Many more examples could be given from the way Police forces now operate to the poor levels of health care in many countries for all except the super wealthy and, even then, it is not as good as it once was.

Perhaps one of the most worrying factors is the poor levels of communication between individuals. Our global culture of greed has reduced any natural communication, unless there is an immediate profit to be realised from it. If there is, people are superficially friendly, at least until the transaction has completed, then they disappear. If there is not, people simply ignore each other as they are glued to their mobile phones. If you say 'hello' to a stranger and smile, they will likely look at you briefly in amazement and hurry away as quickly as they can. If you say hello to a child, their parents will pull them away quickly.

This anti-social behaviour may not occur absolutely everywhere, but it is spreading and it is a worrying development for humankind. We are deliberately being turned into consumer robots. The little the individual knows or understands, the better. Masud has made a point of asking the young people whom he occasionally meets some very basic questions about history, geography or the arts. Even so called 'educated' youngsters have no idea what he is talking about. They have never heard of Beethoven or Charles Dickens. They know nothing of natural processes such as how a tree works or the transformation of dragonflies. They do not understand what was behind the two world wars and have no understanding at all of the Medieval world or later civilisations. Basic scientific knowledge is conspicuous by its absence. These are all topics which would have been considered as 'general knowledge' a few generations back and yet, it seems that youngsters can progress throughout both junior and secondary education without learning anything at all of value. If they continue through to higher education, they can earn an arts degree without any effort at all. A science degree is not much better as they will simply copy information from the Internet in order to put something together for their thesis, which will consequently have nothing original in it at all. With the advent of artificial intelligence and the fact that nearly all publishing has moved to America, this will ensure that would be students can write their various dissertations almost automatically.

This is a disaster for humanity as it means that the vast majority of even 'educated' individuals have no real education at all because they have no understanding of the subject matter at hand. Of course, there are exceptions and some students will learn their subject matter, although probably nothing outside of it. Most just learn how to pass exams. Then they go out into the world and get highly paid jobs as lawyers, doctors or pretend scientists. Even engineers have little knowledge compared with just a few generations back, as they rely upon computers to make calculations for them.

The almost total reliance upon computers is another huge backwards step for civilisation as it continues the dumbing down process. Modern doctors seem incapable of any diagnosis without a computer. How can this be after years of study? It is because during their years of study they have learned very little indeed. They have no ability to think on their feet and to diagnose intelligently. They cannot prescribe any drug or recommend any treatment without referencing a computer. This is, of course, exactly what the computer and software industry want. For everyone, including so called professionals, to be helpless without a computer. For non professionals, the mobile phone or tablet device forms the same purpose. If youngsters suddenly lose access to their mobile phones, they are completely helpless because they have not learned how to function in life without them. Many businesses and utilities also rely absolutely upon mobile communication devices and computers.

This situation is particularly dangerous as it means that whoever controls these infrastructures controls the world. Civilisations may be brought down at the flick of a switch. Do we think that malicious countries would not do this? We once thought that no-one would drop an atomic bomb.

All of these things and indeed this very book, point towards the fact that global civilisation is sliding backwards at an alarming rate, led mostly by one country. The associated definition of the term 'humanity' has consequently been changed and manipulated by the evildoers and the greedy. Yes, it remains in the hearts of a good many individuals around the world but their proportionality is shrinking. This of course is the intention of the global powers who manipulate and control the culture of greed, ensuring that new generations grow up thinking that all this is normal and that there is nothing to worry about. It is not normal and we should be extremely worried, especially for the wellbeing of our children and grandchildren.

The evildoers have already ensured that the vast majority of youngsters around the world grow up with virtually no knowledge or understanding. They believe everything they are told and move with the herd, as intended. Give them a mobile phone, drugs and lots of violent movies and computer games and they will be happy enough. But this is a recipe for disaster somewhere further along the line.

Some countries believe that they are immune from all this because they are currently wealthy and enjoy a higher standard of living. They are not immune. They are simply living in a bubble as they too depend upon the same infrastructures and their youngsters, while better educated, remain uneducated in the broader sense. They have no idea of world history or any deep understanding of the sciences.

The world has become largely dependent upon one country. It consumes its products, uses its infrastructure and copies its so called 'cultural' ideas, including the global culture of greed. The problem with this is that the country concerned has absolutely no moral code or sense of responsibility towards humanity.

Indeed, it never has done. It has no understanding or concept of ethics and has been shown to be treacherous and to distort and manipulate the truth on countless occasions. For the world to pattern itself upon this culture is asking for trouble and, indeed, we can see some of this trouble erupting in the world today. It is shrouded in outright lies and media manipulation in an attempt to justify the unjustifiable. Some see through this, but most do not because they have already been conditioned by the system.

One of the dangers inherent in this approach is, should the masses finally wake up, there will be large scale trouble all around the world. And this will not be as simple as one country against another, it will be an international reaction to covert tyranny which will likely bring everything to a halt. Could global civilisation recover from such an event? perhaps, but not without an enormous amount of destruction and loss of life. Furthermore, humankind will not possess the necessary skills with which to rebuild its own civilisation. This places it upon a very slippery slope towards the last day.

None of this is new. It was predicted by the ancient Egyptians in some detail and is referenced in subsequent scriptures. When shall humanity wake up and re-establish itself? It may be accomplished yet, but only if we act swiftly. There is much more that could be said here but, suffice it to say, that the concept of humanity is currently under threat.

Masud thanks the readers of this and his other four books and hopes that, taken together, they bring with them enlightenment for the young and some comfort for older generations in that they are not alone. There exists a silent minority who do understand these things. However, they need to teach others and, in particular, the younger generations who have been so mercilessly manipulated by the in place systems. So, do please pass on details of Masud's works and encourage others to read for themselves and, hopefully, to be inspired towards the straight path and the truth. From such a position, they may carve a better life for themselves.

Alhamdulillah

www.ingramcontent.com/pod-product-compliance
Lightning Source LLC
Chambersburg PA
CBHW061046250726
48653CB00001B/280